crunch

an ode.
to crisps

CRUNCH

ff

natalie
whittle

First published in 2024
by Faber & Faber Limited
The Bindery, 51 Hatton Garden
London EC1N 8HN

Typeset by Faber & Faber Limited
Printed and bound by CPI Group (UK) Ltd, Croydon, CR0 4YY

A CIP record for this book
is available from the British Library

ISBN 978-0-571-38410-5

MIX
Paper | Supporting
responsible forestry
FSC® C171272
FSC
www.fsc.org

Printed and bound in the UK on FSC® certified paper in line with our continuing
commitment to ethical business practices, sustainability and the environment.
For further information see faber.co.uk/environmental-policy

2 4 6 8 10 9 7 5 3 1

For Emma, Mayanthi and Angela,
and for more crisps together

contents

prologue: to a crisp

Some people remember holiday food. I remember holiday crisps.

Before I explain why, and before I begin this tale, I admit there is no photo album to open at an explanatory time and place.

There is no latitude, no longitude, no true beginning. I have always and I will always love crisps.

As cashiers check banknotes, I hold each crisp up to the light and admire its soak of industrial, golden oil, wondering at its unrepeatable, fried imperfections. A raw potato slice, now creatively misshapen and curled. All the while, I anticipate the crunch.

Most obsessions end. But this one replenishes itself. I will keep eating crisps, and yet they will never diminish. By the time I reach the bottom hem of a packet, crumbs and splinters are there, but they are not the end of anything. And no matter that I can never own a bag of crisps – only buy and eat them – I will have possession of another bag of crisps in my future. I am always preparing to eat more.

Which is to say that I suppose, in a way, in their own small way, crisps are part of what I live for.

Now, if, when reading this confession about crisps, you feel that we have something in common, this book will hopefully be a companion to you, as a dedicated crisp fan. Your reading will be a companion to me, too, in the moments when I feel alone on a craggy crisp island. But if learning that I live for crisps makes you think we are different, or makes you hope that we are different, the following pages may be curious.

Regardless, it is hard to escape the strange connective force of crisps in British life. They punctuate workdays and complete meal deals and they bridge the hunger gap between afternoons and evenings. They go well with vices, surprise dull sandwiches and, in dire circumstances, they are just enough to sustain us. They're well travelled, but vanish before the destination, crunched away between cities and towns and backwaters and bus stops. They slip unscathed in and out of different social classes, at once supremely ordinary, and underrated for their weirdness. Until I wrote this book, I had never tried to explain to myself how or why a 1970s dinner-party dish became my favourite crisp flavour. I was too busy enjoying my prawn cocktail reverie.

But before I go too much further into these crisp matters, and hopefully unravel the mystery of prawn cocktail, let me start this tale again, on a campsite in Brittany, on an unnamed day of my childhood, inside a memory that has more brain fog around it than light.

I start again here because I can see parts of it clearly. It is where something stuck. Where some clusters of neurons unexpectedly met French crisps. The beginning, perhaps, of a slight curling to something that had previously been flat. The Old English *crisp*, for curly, came from the Latin *crispus*, for curled. Here was a kink in the line of reason.

prologue

To reach Brittany we had set off in the night, driving the head-lamps through the bends of the lanes, heading from Wales for the Channel crossing at dawn. The car, a small steel tin in the dark, had a deep silvery coldness to it, as if we were driving across the moon in our sleeping bags.

Hours trundling west the next day through France brought out large leg rashes from the now-suffocating foam seats, sprawling red on our skin like new French birthmarks. But then at Camping Les Pins, our feet finally warm on the ground, came the old pine smell of French summer. The campsite was near the Iroise Sea below Crozon, and it belonged to an 'almost island', or 'presque-isle', where a sliver of land was just a few hundred thousand millennia from breaking off the mainland into the Atlantic. The French called it the *presqu'île au bout du monde*, but it felt like a safe and gentle place. A sweetness radiated from the salt winds through the branches. Something good was here.

Rattling poles and faded canvas from the car boot became our bell tent, and a washing line between tree trunks dried our towels. We started spending our pocket-money francs liberally at the *boulangerie*, a tempting short walk from the campsite, and we sat and swam for a few sunburnt days at the beaches.

Over this first intoxicating stretch as a temporarily Gallic eight-year-old, I began to hold a trust in Brittany's foodstuffs that felt electric, a confidence that French superiority was guaranteed over almost every item we'd eaten before at home.

The large crispy pancakes, the golden baguettes and the butter biscuits in our picnics, but also the nutty cheese in the pancakes, the salty butter on the bread, the big almonds studded into the biscuit fingers: all had unmasked the British equivalents as impostors in boxes, sad cardboard hollows, propping up a flimsy but evidently organised supermarket lie.

About a week into the holiday, after another day shuttling between the *boulangerie* and the beach, my sisters and I were in the everlasting middle of a card game, our parents drinking in silence. (This was the 1980s.) The warmth was unevening in the pines around our tent, the light going out. Nonetheless, we expected this day to close like a triumphant sunset. Any minute now, we would be allowed to open the thing we had whined tenaciously for: a giant red mega-sack of *chips de pommes de terre*. We would get what we wanted. We would eat foreign crisps.

And now, opening the 'cheeps' from the French *supermarché*, we had a chance to compare something we already knew well against this revelatory culinary standard. What superior way, we wanted to know, would the French have with the potato?

The adults looked askance as we crammed splintering fistfuls into our faces for the answer. We were hungry and greedy, but curious too. The potato slices? Thinner, flatter, more translucent, held up to the fading Breton light. The cooking? Less oily. Salt? Maybe less of it than an average packet back home. And wasn't the potato itself different, tasting more of elegant France than of dumpy Britain, somehow? It was less earthy, less like the memory of soil on potato skin hadn't fully washed off. (The classically pale colour of French crisps wasn't in my imagination – European crisp makers sometimes use destarched and blanched potato varieties, which do produce whiter slices.)

In the campsite at dusk, an argument soon broke out. Who had eaten more than their fair share? This was harder to determine since the French didn't approach crisps twenty-five grams at a time, in one-person packets. Instead they sold cash-and-carry-size sacks almost a kilo in weight, sorted into only two or three flavours – salt, paprika and sour cream and chive. Even a corner shop in Britain would stock a minimum of twenty varieties to avoid embarrassment. It was also never explained why the French didn't sell crisps in smaller portions, but this just added to our endorsement.

For a child, all these unanswered questions made 'les chips' essential investigative eating for the short evenings before we were packed into our tent to argue on by torchlight, waking up the next morning with our hands of cards paused under our camp pillows. My parents sipped on through their wine, holiday-deaf to our squabbles.

A week after our first French crisps, we pulled up the tent pegs and headed, with more freckles and more fat, for the Cherbourg ferry. I felt buoyed by having discovered the secret existence of French food. But I returned home with a concurrent feeling: a loyalty to the comparative silliness of British crisps; an allegiance to a quality that demanded unthinking acceptance that potato snacks could imitate limitless flavours for fun, or wear their extruded shapes as humans do Halloween costumes, to produce a salt and vinegar flying saucer, for example, or a pickled onion monster foot. The reciprocity of this understanding was comforting. And perhaps, related to this feeling, I also returned home nursing a small perverse guilt for my abandonment of the harmless mediocrity of the British diet, too. By the end of the holiday the straightforwardness of French crisps had made me a little homesick – crispsick, even – for the imperfections of life on the other side of the Channel. Briefly, crisps had made me a patriot.

Almost every country I've visited since has proffered some take on the potato crisp. Crisps are like a global currency that waxes and wanes in value as you tour the world, with Lay's available almost everywhere, like a fried-potato dollar. It has become a cardinal act of tourism to buy a packet of crisps on arrival in a new place, and find my bearings (sometimes judgements) through the contents.

Often, the better a country's food culture, the less compensatory flair you'll find in the crisp aisle. Italy, for example, has its huge dreamlike vocabulary of pasta shapes and sauces, but as a nation it speaks only a few dismissive words of crisp flavourings. France is beginning to catch up (I highly recommend Brets Jura cheese flavour) but the richness and balance of French food culture have traditionally worked around the urge for frenzied kaleidoscopes of crisps. (I remember when my French school exchange partner explained at her home in the Paris suburbs that she and indeed all French people did not eat between meals, an announcement that impressed and then disappointed me when it became clear she wasn't lying.)

Some countries strive for and achieve impressive mimicry of national dishes – Patatas Torres' uncanny Spanish fried egg-flavoured crisps come to mind first in this category – but the accuracy can taste unpalatable, or feel like an advertisement of your strangerhood. Canada likes its poutine and lobster crisps, while the Belgians enjoy theirs pickle- and burger-flavoured. Mexico is so famous for its sizzling diet that its enthusiasm for crisps is not well publicised, yet they come salt-and-lime-flavoured, in *fuego* and *flamas* chilli heats, rolled up like mini tortilla cigars and generally made with creative snack abandon. Asia's astounding food flair is more than matched in its system of crisps, in which seemingly no order is too tall: salted egg, fried crab, roasted fish – the flavours of anything beloved can be plucked there for a potato.

This is the thing about crisps: they're a conjuring spell – suspend disbelief to imagine this potato is actually a fried egg – but the point is not for the potato to taste exactly like the egg, or the crab, but rather to see how close it can get.

There is no egg in Torres' fried egg crisp, but it is celebrated for its egginess. Patatas Torres, a family-run crisper that began life in a factory outside Barcelona in 1969, told me that the egg flavour is derived from a 'natural aroma' that mimics the real thing almost perfectly, and is widely talked about for doing so. Not long ago I attended a Thanksgiving party in Dublin at which the American host's deliciously homemade pumpkin pie was upstaged in conversation by a bag of Torres fried egg crisps that had been brought by an Irish guest. (Ireland has a big heart for crisps, as I will explore later.)

It's almost as if the departure of the UK from the European Union has made European crisp makers more British in our absence. Patatas Torres says bolder flavours are doing good business in the traditionally crisp-conservative Spanish domestic market. 'The target of our "flavoured" potato chips is broadening,' they explained. 'There has been a great development as far as the attitude of our consumers is concerned. They are more receptive towards the idea of trying flavours that can highly surprise them.' Another premium crisper, the Belgian-owned but 'made in Madrid' branded Superbon, has begun to filter into British delis, smattering shelves with the likes of seaweed and yellow paprika flavours. On the streets of Madrid, it's not uncommon to see crisps heaped like hotel cornflakes in the windows of shops that specialise in crisps, dried fruits and nuts. They are shovelled into bags fresh to order, usually plain or salted, and fried in olive oil.

Flavour allows for contradictions as well as surprises – while writing this I just ate a packet of Asian BBQ pulled pork crisps from Marks & Spencer, which bears the footnote 'suitable for vegetarians' on the back of the packet. The potato has been flavoured to not just be a potato, but the pork flavour is also not pork. For the ultimate meta flavour, just open a tube of Pringles loaded baked potato: potato flavouring (plus bacon, cheese and chilli flavouring) piled on to a slice of extruded potato flour. Dehydrations of real flavours – a Cheddar cheese, for example – are meanwhile lauded for their authenticity, even if the amount used is minuscule.

Crisps are the most pleasurable, multi-dimensional and seemingly harmless source of deceit. I even admit to enjoying the false promise I make to myself when opening a big packet and vowing not to eat it all in one go. It's a lie: of course I won't have the self-restraint, but the little crumb of its possibility tastes good.

prologue

When I began to write this book, I also semi-promised myself: not too many crisps. The halving of resolve always sounds a warning: it is a bell tolling somewhere that the goal I've set myself is already out of time. The other day I found myself in the local deli, in search of new crisps. I picked up a bag of Torres pickle and onion, a flavour that satisfied the 'Is this research?' test because it's imported from Spain and I had not seen it anywhere else. The man behind the counter said it was his favourite flavour, most likely to trigger his 'lizard brain' instinct, a signal to override the stop button. I nodded, sympathetically, as if I was yet to be struck by this weakness.

But even as I crave them, I realise a pouch of potato chips is a kind of meanness, as much as a repeated abundance. A bag of crisps is half air, half product, and brevity is inbuilt, as if the little rectangle is all but designed to breed my want. Crisps are flavoured, but odourless, and have none of the cooking aroma that is a social part of eating, in which the guests at a table share anticipation through their nostrils. Sometimes when I look at a bowl of crisps I think I can smell the oil and salt, but it is my habit that has grafted aromatic perception onto a visual. Multipack bags of crisps are only five grams heavier than the reduced chocolate rations handed to surveilled citizens in George Orwell's nightmare, *Nineteen Eighty-Four*. Is twenty-five grams all our appetite is worth? Are crisps enough?

At home, growing up, crisps were a 5 p.m. feature. Around this time, our boxy white television was switched on with a frisk of electricity across the screen, reanimating the saga of the Melbourne suburbs. We crunched through packets of Walkers smoky bacon, still wearing our school uniforms, committed like sports fans to the outcome of Kylie Minogue and Jason Donovan's love affair.

In between classroom lessons and bedroom homework, a period of precious self-zombification was granted by this free-form crisp hour. The flavouring distribution of smoky bacon was particularly intense, making it like an ingenious sandpaper that could be grated across the tongue while also following the sub-plots in Australia. With the crisp suspended on my taste buds, the fake bacon almost started to fizz as it was absorbed, doing something unknown but welcome to the receptors in my brain.

'Stop scronching,' my oldest sister used to say from her prime TV spot, as I progressed through the packet.

'I'm not,' I replied, an honest answer that I believed spoke to the unfair acoustic judgements that pass between siblings on their eating habits. But in my own head, I relished the volume of the crunch: louder than my own thoughts, but at the same time not deafening, crisp-crunching was like the temporary absence of a burden. (Researchers since at least the 1980s have been establishing the link between auditory cues and perception of quality and crispness in potato chips.) Inasmuch as all addictions are post-ponements, my fixation on crisps was about a total replacement of one state with another. Its brevity didn't matter. Through food, it was possible to feel differently.

We repeated this routine – school, home, crisps, arguments – for much of our childhood. In our house that sat by a damp old railway bank, just beyond vegetable allotments, towards even damper farmhouses and forgotten cottages, the virulence of our crisp-based disputes at least gave us something to talk about. The memory of campsite crisps, and the sunshine of Breton life in general, receded into the slow progress of a child's year – summer would take forever to come around again.

In the arena of other people's houses, where as guests our behavioural standards had to rise, the presence of soft, clean carpets underfoot immediately signalled that we were in a zone of politeness. Instead of verbal assaults, my sisters and I chided each other with angry looks over our favourite territorial skirmish, the crisp allocation.

'You've had more than me,' we scowled wordlessly at each other as the adults gossiped. What's worse, our hosts often had much 'nicer' crisps, the posh kind you got from Marks & Spencer food halls, with convincing and interesting flavours, tastefully crinkle-cut and presented in wincingly small bowls. Restraint was agony.

At the edge of nowhere there was plenty of time for unseen greed. We had three television channels in English and one in Welsh (Channel 4 required a satellite dish), scant social life and a telephone with a sticker on the receiver that asked, in my father's handwriting: 'Who is paying for this phone call?'

On my bicycle rides down the lane, the hedgerows of hazel, bindweed, blackberry, dogwood, nettles and orchard grass grew high enough in summer to hide the rest of the world. Sometimes I would stop to talk to the farmer, Ike, who lived in the farmhouse a few fields along the lane. He cycled between sheep fields perennially wearing a cloth hat, which he removed as a sign he expected a conversation. Ike had a long frizzy beard, and talked with ease about death and the Second World War. I suspected, listening to him with the bicycle chains ticking, that my childhood was caught somewhere that wasn't the fullest present day. All the more I craved the products that were democratically modern – new and the same everywhere, available everywhere. Crisps included. Crisps especially.

This, the 1980s, was the decade in which going back or forward in cultural time demanded watchful patience. Winding album cassettes and video tapes to precise starts and stops was its own art form, and the best TV movies were waited for like Sunday buses. The general present tense was dictated by where you lived – usually, if you did not live in a big city, you felt not years behind but years away, as if the future was simply happening without you. Phoning the speaking clock, in which national time was narrated minute by minute from a tape synched to the Royal Greenwich Observatory, was one of my favourite pastimes.

Perhaps because of the enclosure this created, and the limited understanding of childhood, I had a conviction that crisps actually *belonged* to the 1980s – as if Scampi Fries and crispy bacon Frazzles were naturally the way we lived now, but also a shortcut to catch up with what we were missing. My misconceptions included total ignorance of the fact that crisps had been for sale since at least the 1920s, and that their popularity had since circumnavigated the globe from San Antonio, Texas all the way to Tokyo, Japan.

The war my farmer neighbour Ike was preoccupied by in our

chats had also spurred many crisp companies into being during the scrambling of peacetime recovery. In the UK alone, many hundreds of crisp companies had already been and gone by the 1940s – crisped briefly, and then went limp. Paiges Potato Crisp Limited, for example, wound up in 1930. Lennard's Crisps Limited, dissolved 1932. Krunch Potato Crisps Limited, dissolved in 1948. Who remembers these long-lost attempts at crisp glory?

Your own crisp references may be different – earlier, later – but with the same inevitable tangle of nostalgia. Colson Whitehead observed in his post-9/11 essay 'The Colossus of New York' that you become a New Yorker at the moment when the laundromat that used to stand on the street corner is more real than the coffee shop that stands there now. The physical vanishings themselves are impermanent, thanks to the powers of human memory. Every new person to arrive in the city has some different marker for what used to be where, Whitehead wrote, and this collective jumble of time and longing brings the city folds of criss-crossed character. Some of this translates to branded goods. My lost love – my weird, beloved Walkers Worcestershire sauce – might not be the same as yours (does anyone miss Walkers lamb and mint?), but we inhabit the same fondness for a crisp out of reach.

A debate on this theme ricocheted through the letters pages of the *Financial Times* back in 1985. One J. R. Phelps first wrote to the editor to observe that potato crisps then were not what they were before the war, in the 1930s. Other correspondents pitched in to agree and disagree in a volley of letters until J. R. Cullip, marketing director of Walkers Crisps, wrote a definitive-sounding rebuttal to the original claim. The pre-war crisp, Cullip suggested, was 'almost certainly rancid', and damp salt and un-crisp staleness were in fact regular hazards of Phelps's supposed halcyon crisp days – unlike, he noted, the Walkers crisp of his present day, 1985, which was 'a Prince, nay a King, in comparison': freshly made, airtight, consistent year-round and still inflation-beating good value, he added.

What's striking about this to me is how adamant Cullip was about the princely superiority of the then-contemporary Walkers. He writes as if he was not around to taste what Phelps had, but dismisses the product as 'almost certainly rancid'. Almost certainly, there was some evidence to back up such swagger, but part of this book's mission is to probe the extent to which we can judge or evaluate the differences and betterments between eras in which our absence is the firmest and most vivid truth. Indeed, in ex-Walkers chief executive Martin Glenn's 'video book' *The Best Job in the World*, he notes that see-through plastic crisp packets, which didn't help the freshness of crisps, were only phased out by the company in favour of shiny foil upgrades in 1992. The addition of a nitrogen flush, he goes on, to prevent oxidisation, didn't happen at Walkers until 1996. I think the ready salted crisps that I eat today are as good as the ones I ate as a child. But I am not entirely certain. And as for the pre-war crisp, I do not know.

In the need-more, never-enough domain of crisp eating, one packet would generally only serve to highlight a problem, rather than resolve my hunger. The grams of a Walkers packet could be eked out to last through some of *Neighbours* and into *Home and Away*, but then the silver foil stared back, and beyond this point, there were very good-bad rituals. Open up the packet and lick the salt and flavour crumbs. Attempt a gullet-catching instead, tipping your head back for the last cascade of tiny sharded pieces. Go in search of another hit, but be prepared for shame. 'You'll spoil your dinner,' our parents used to say, their motto for almost any food consumed after breakfast.

When school friends came over, hospitality of course involved crisps. But to truly impress a guest, there was also a high theatrical manoeuvre – the shrinking of the crisp packets. First (don't try this at home, the formula of the bags has changed – maybe crisp companies realised what children were doing), we smoothed them flat like sacrificial sleeping bags on a baking tray. Then we placed them in a hot oven, and stood by watching while the packets bubbled and drew air into themselves until, magically, they shrank. What was particularly satisfying about this procedure was that the designs and colours and logos were unharmed by the heat – perhaps a little wonky overall, but what emerged was in essence a tiny facsimile packet. I loved the smell of furred hot plastic, too, with its satisfying whiff of danger averted.

In fact, the flexible entertainment potential seemed to be the very point of crisps, once a stolid bag of potatoes, now a starting point for fun. Hula Hoops were almost a bespoke circumference for a child's fingers, and I discovered the delight of wearing them on both hands as ceremonial crisp rings, then eating them one by one by cracking my teeth over the digits.

A plain sandwich could be crispified with a crunchy layer of ready salted inserted and pressed down to crackle under the bread. Enough Wotsits turned your tongue a sick, brilliant orange. Chopsticks had a peculiar quality whereby you could create one giant (and revolting) bolus of chewed potato flour in your mouth, welding the sticks together. Pickled onion Monster Munch made the sides of your face wince with a thunderbolt of sourness. Old-fashioned Smith's came with a pleasingly tiny blue packet of salt that you sprinkled and shook to taste, as if the chief executive had deferred this important decision to you, a minor. Each crisp had personality and precise cultural identity, which when assembled into a supermarket category added up to a soothing offer of variety, as if the length of the snack aisle was a sure distance in which to find your mood cured or reflected back to you, somewhere.

If you're unfamiliar with this territory in British life, you may already be starting to ask: is there something wrong with this person? In my defence, I can confidently say I am not the only one who displayed the crisp commitment. My memory is of lots of children revelling in crisps just as much as I did. Crisp jewellery was great, foreign crisps were interesting, crisp-packet shrinking felt inspired. The sheer variety of crisp eating – melting prawn cocktail Skips, brittle bacon Frazzles – combined with the sub-breeds of snacks that weren't classical crisps, such as Scampi Fries and Pringles, made the pursuit an odyssey. Nobody under the age of twelve would argue against it.

The crisp world continues to be a jungle. Under the canopy of potato products, there is a teeming mass of other sub-crisp species. Pork puffs. Chickpea curls. Lentil chips. Popped cheesies. Crunchy corn. Kosher wheat twists. Seaweed wafers. They all belong together, as part of the wider snack ecosystem.

Except in the view of His Majesty's Revenue and Customs, which greets different classes of product with a spectrum of more or less appealing taxes. Remember the semantic confusion that exploded when Procter & Gamble, owner of the Pringles brand, successfully pleaded to the British High Court that Pringles were not in fact potato chips, and thereby exempt from VAT, but subsequently lost the case in 2009 at the Court of Appeal? The court ruled that Pringles satisfied two tests: they were similar to potato crisps, and they were made from the potato (at least 40 per cent of their ingredients were, at least). It comes back to the tax distinction between food for subsistence and food for luxury, a point that separates the zero-rated from the VAT-ed, but also a distinction that is pertinent to this book more broadly. Whether or not crisps are basic, or brilliant, or luxurious, is a question I will address throughout.

All this preceded the tidal wave of nutritional education that swept crisp culture away from 'child's paradise' towards a bleaker landscape of 'consume in moderation'. The shelves of the local Spar used to pad out row upon row with individual crisp packets, plumped up neatly like fluorescent artillery. There were no warnings, no glaring calorie counts, no traffic lights for fat and heart attacks. Though it was clear that crisps weren't the finest foodstuffs and no health match for a blameless apple or banana, we didn't live with the pill of national knowledge, disseminated through doctors' surgeries and television adverts. To a 1980s child, public health was about as relevant as a bank building.

Crucially, crisp companies made the most of this moment by devising all their products as if they were children themselves. They understood, earlier than most industries, the capital potential of a child's sometimes strange desire for escape. It wasn't just about coming up with a good flavour; it was also about satisfying a child's natural and brutal intelligence by doing something unimpeachably and recognisably clever. Good crisps were the acme of humour, imagination and fun; food technology was only one part of the puzzle.

Something about this approach was peculiarly British. As we found in the supermarkets of Brittany, French food manufacturers weren't that bothered about signing up children to a crisp religion that would separate them from their pocket money. They were too busy feeding them 'real' food, not needing the crutch of powdered flavour. British food manufacturers were in on a different game, one that proved hugely lucrative, and drew a path towards a new British diet fed by fun, but dangerously carefree (perhaps careless) about health. For me, this has lasted a lifetime. On the special occasions when my childhood home filled with people for holiday-slideshow dinners, the role the children played happily was to circle the room as crisp waiting staff, pacing from person to person with a bowl as the Kodak pictures clicked onto the projector. At parties now the sight of crisp bowls beckons to me, through habit, like the face of a person I know. Good crisp routines have meanwhile been repeated into entitlements: crisps as the ritual before family dinners and nights out, crisps as the small cheer of train rides, and crisps as the small consolation of countless hurried lunch breaks.

When I first joined the *Financial Times* in a junior pool of night-shift sub-editors, a misfitting newspaper world began to colour itself in. I discovered the evening canteen served some glorious steamed puddings, but also superbly eccentric salads. You could withdraw cash, exchange coins and buy stamps from machines on the top floor, like a cross between a post office and a casino. By way of befriendment amid the confusion, my desk neighbour Dennis offered me cigars at our 10 p.m. dinner breaks. Nothing made perfect sense to me, except for the sound of the managing editor – an old-fashioned and brilliant newspaper man – banging furious fists on the vending machine when he found it empty of salt and vinegar just before his planned nightly escape to the smoking room.

I am not the only person to have a thing with crisps. The how and why of this is traceable not just through my own or a British national character but also along the lines of industry, agriculture and the twentieth century's gift for brands and marketing. At one point in my twenties I even created a Facebook group called 'Crisps Anonymous', to explore the compulsive ability to eat crisps by our body weight. (People joined, but a few others laughed, and eventually I archived it in shame.)

Are Brits the leaders globally when it comes to consuming snacks? Far from it. By one measure at least, the global crown of snacking belongs to Japan, where in 2022 per-capita volume sales amounted to thirty-four kilos, way ahead of the UK at just over five and a half kilos in the same year. (Snacks in this data set included cookies and crackers, potato chips, tortilla chips, flips and pretzels.) In the $98 billion market for potato chips alone, the greatest revenue share is generated in the US, where sales were forecast to reach $33 billion in 2024. The point of difference is that the UK regards crisps almost as a national dish, a proprietary part of Britishness, as if the blue and green packets of cheese and onion and salt and vinegar meant as much patriotically as the red breast of a postbox.

The salty siren works at all ages, across all demographics, Pom-Bears to Quavers and Kettle Chips. Not exactly a social leveller, but not an exclusive commodity, either. Picture a train carriage speeding between UK towns on a weekend and you'll see them in the gallery of locomotive faces, the crisp eaters, entranced by the journey and a crisp packet, hands like soft claws drifting among crumbs, headphones on, going somewhere. A British bliss.

For a dark week in November 2021, the depth of the affair was revealed when it was broken off. There was a brief but nationwide crisp shortage, prompted by a faulty IT upgrade at the Walkers factory in Leicestershire. The software problem stopped the factory from producing all but its classic flavours (ready salted, salt and vinegar, cheese and onion), creating in the process a national downturn in supply, as crisp eaters turned to other brands and effectively bought out the entire British inventory of crisps. The Walkers factory, among the world's largest devoted to the manufacture of crisps, is ordinarily a peerless academy of potato-chip expertise: processing, flavour, logistics. The 'crisis' was picked up on in the news, and gently ridiculed. How embarrassing, but also how endearing, the headlines implied, for a nationwide anxiety to be provoked by something as trifling as crisps.

Loving crisps is one of the most abundant things the British do economically – tens of millions of packets are sold every day. The wholesale margins are not lavish, at about 30 per cent, rising for big sharing bags, and so it follows that crisps can be relied upon to be wedged in all the places we might be tempted by them – any train station, supermarket, pub or corner shop will place them at eye level to catch our passing fancy. Generations of specialist crisp-potato farmers have been kept in business as a result, and the UK has emerged with the world-beating, aforementioned Walkers factory in Leicester.

Yet between the curls of crisps, there are invisibilities. Crisps reward the least glamorous of the business traits above all: organisation, meticulous planning and engagement in ruthless competition. It is telling that only a handful of fully independent crispers exist in today's UK market – Kent Crisps, in the garden of England, survives partly by staying small, with seven flavours and a modest £1.5m turnover (see page 200). It's also a rare crisp company in the UK to be run by a woman as sole director.

And of course, as soon as a nation has a cipher, it exposes itself to the revelation of its good, bad and most human sides. Crisps represent British humour, and a flair for invention. But on a number of occasions, they've been props in more serious drama. The ability to open and consume a packet of crisps is synonymous with the ability to control grip and fine motor skills, a banal gesture of 'day-to-day activities' that becomes volatile when debated in certain legal contexts. The annals of British case law are littered with mentions of crisp packets, like the aftermath of a particularly chaotic party. Per the records of court hearings, judges have heard how crisps were stolen, how they were left abandoned on pallets for months waiting for import paperwork to be filled, how tubs of them were smashed in anger as preludes to violence, how they provided solace for the infirm and vulnerable, how they were given as parenting bribes in custody disputes, and how they were remembered as part of the incidental fabric of days overshadowed by life-altering trauma.

What follows in this book is an attempt to understand what I was oblivious to as a child – that crisps are a complicated novelty. And I am interested in the way crisps are an activated product – how they need crisp eaters to create the crunch, otherwise they would not be crisp at all: they would be unheard, uncrunched, stale and eventually soft inside unopened bags. Crisps need actors to come to life. What kind of theatre does that make us?

This book's path for answers is through national identities, science, social structures, business cultures and British life, as much as through a thread of my own memories and curiosity. I'll try, somewhat, not to eat too many as I write (let's assume Chapter 1 resets this vow to zero), and I'll seek to correct assumptions that I have already made, since really not everything is as it seems in the world of sliced potatoes.

Prepare a bowl of your choice for the social history of crisps. Prepare to crunch.

1

very plain

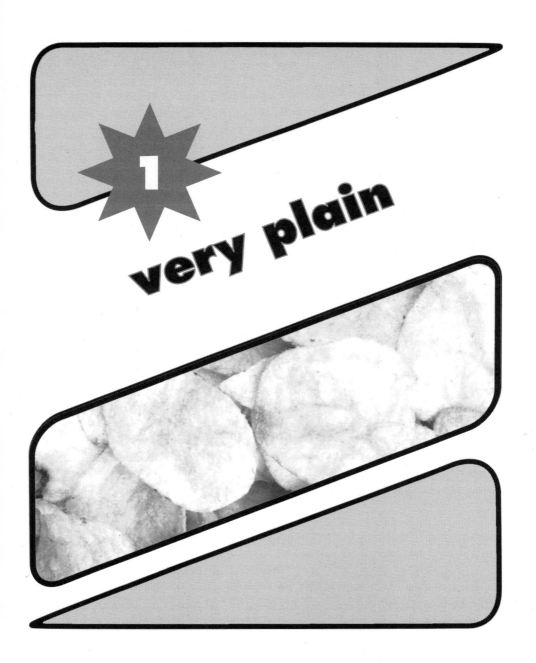

Arlington Business Park, like business parks anywhere, is close to a roaring main road. In this case, it is barely half a mile from Junction 12 of the M4 in West Berkshire, eleven motorway chunks from London.

Sitting at the edge of Theale parish, flung off a big roundabout, Arlington Business Park is also close to something vanished – a seventeenth-century stagecoach route that once paused at coaching inns in the village for hay, brown ale and dim meaty dinners. Travellers may also have faced ladles of soupy cabbage, but probably not potatoes. Potatoes would take a few more generations for us to eat them unthinkingly like bread, and inevitably, to take them more or less for granted.

In a building of glass and chrome that stares at an artificial lake, Arlington was for a long time the headquarters address of Walkers Snack Food Limited, staffed by hundreds of sales and admin personnel in a blunt corporate appendix to village life. Recently, Walkers HQ left and moved east – to a very similar building in Green Park Business Park outside Reading, a nudge further along the M4.

Walkers began just after the Second World War in Leicester, to the north, and for its first few decades it was a local business, rarely crossing the unwritten border to the South of England, which itself is the unmarked gateway to global trade. Today, Walkers is a national brand name, in control of one of the biggest crisp factories in the world. And its Southern offices, in the money belt that cinches around London, mean Walkers can now make an agricultural sign of the cross from its strategic crisp zones in the UK, touching seed-potato supplier farms in Scotland, tracing down to the Green Park desk jobs, over and up to Coventry, where the brand's owner PepsiCo makes many of its snacks and sugary drinks, and back across to the bursting-with-crisps heart, the main prideful Leicester factory, near some of the best crisping-potato farmers in the country.

I know all this. Except whenever I open a bag of Walkers, I know absolutely nothing of this. I do not stop to check the best before date, which Walkers swears is always a Saturday, since its factory production week starts on Sundays, and all crisps made that week take the same 'best before end' stamp. (Crisps generally last about three months: longer if they're made from preserved potato flakes or double sealed in tins.) I forget about the potato purchasers, trend forecasters, potato-transport bulkers, waste compactors, factory machinery, potato breeders and flavour makers. Phones in offices do not ring about potato pricing, and no one has ever sent an email about prawn cocktail. I ignore it all.

When the crisp bag opens, with its short exhalation of cushioning air, it is the last time that the potatoes inside see daylight. I do not dwell on how they reached me from the darkness underground, or how they've come to taste convincingly like faraway things such as red Thai chillies. I do not measure the distance between myself and the factory door. I only know how close the crisp is to my eating.

However, since this book seeks the full crisp experience – the abstract parts as much as the edible ones – I have tried not to look away from the things that might otherwise be blanks. And to begin this unblindfolding, there's one detail I have learned that I always think about when I eat a bag of crisps, which is the crisp makers' rule about golf courses.

At least one large manufacturer of crisps in the United Kingdom, setting terms via its potato merchants, will not accept spuds grown within half a kilometre of a golf course. The same five hundred-metre rule applies to open countryside where golfers are thought to be working on their rough shots. Fields close by are crisping-potato no-go territory.

The reason for the rule relates to common carrion crows, which are not only gifted scavengers but also open-minded enough to pick up almost anything, including stray golf balls. Once their interest has worn off, the crows then drop the balls at will. For potato farmers, this creates a risk.

I spot these crows every morning on my way into the local woodland – a mob of them in summer, one or two in winter – wings tucked on the fingerposts and the bins, poised to fly down for festering treasure. They've become my unexpected augurs of all crisps.

All sorts of rogue items find their way into potato fields: pheasant eggs, which are also spud-like to the unfocused eye, tree branches, stones, acorns and shards of glass. The farmers who supply crisping potatoes in such prodigious quantities – to make enough for the roughly 186,000 tonnes of crisps sold annually in the UK – have to be vigilant of every one of these field hazards, as do the crispers.

After arriving at the typical crisp factory, potato loads are trundled into the hangar on a belt to be checked for potato impersonators. A golf ball spotted among the raw crisp material stops everything. The whole batch will be rejected, and the farmer (or their insurer) will foot the bill for lost crisps.

In the case of a 'crisp scare' that made Central Television news in the summer of 1989, a 'saboteur' was seemingly at work within Smith's crisps factory in Lincoln, contaminating packets with shards of car-windscreen glass, broken curtain rings and pieces of wood. Lincolnshire Police launched an investigation and production was halted altogether as the nationwide inventory of Smith's was recalled for safety. One Smith's worker, interviewed by Central Television, said he hoped the 'culprit' would be found and jailed. The boss of Smith's at the time vowed to install factory-floor cameras. (Theoretically, although it's unlikely, the culprit could have been a crow.)

Crisps have to be tightly processed, because the way in which they are made is a three-minute opera of surreal industrial trans-formation. Skins are peeled with special sandpaper, flavour rains in curtains, crisps churn in giant drums. The oil is continually frying, and flammable, and nothing is left to chance, not least because more than a handful of crisp factories have accidentally burned down.

The golf course edict is faithful to this reality. It recognises the arcane requirements of a product that for all the world looks like an obvious and simple idea, reproducible ad infinitum. Potatoes: grown, sliced, fried. Grown, sliced, fried.

What could be less exhaustible, the thinking goes, than the dumbly reproductive potato, the first thing in *The Martian* that

Matt Damon tried, with success, to grow on Mars using his own human waste as fertiliser? (Even though NASA itself has enthused about Martian soil simulants, Red Planet crisps might not be possible outside of Hollywood. There are toxins that would require heavy soil treatment, and low light exposure at Mars's position in the solar system would make potatoes unhappy.)

Earthbound formulas for potato success are just as finicky, and delicately inconstant, depending on the odds of the sun (not too much) and the rain (just enough), the soil (beware pests) and the dramatic ingenuity of the natural world (see the crows). One potato farmer told me he checks the weather on his phone all day 'like the horoscopes' until he finds a forecast that puts his nerves at ease.

Humans, of course, keep complicating matters. The war in Ukraine has limited the supply of sunflower oil, forcing a switch in some places to frying crisps in rapeseed, canola or safflower alternatives. The fierce droughts of changing climates have also left manufacturers with the deeper threat of native potato tonnage deficit.

This kind of problem is existential if you're a Great British crisp brand. For example, is it a sin to bulk out your supply with potatoes shipped in from Europe or Egypt? How many potato slices need to be from British soil? Back-of-packet boasts about British provenance certainly wouldn't be possible in the same way.

The supply of spuds is also doubly fragile, since the potatoes themselves can't just be any old potatoes. For crisps, they must be low-sugar, starchier, and smaller, rounder spuds than those grown for fresh supermarket bags or chipping machines, a shape that slices neatly into doubloons.

To achieve this, crisping potatoes are carefully and secretively bred by plant geneticists in laboratories, time-consuming work that is then patented like any other part of a brand. Open-market varieties, which crisp manufacturers use more sparingly, have characterful names like bookies' favourites – Rooster, Hermes, Atlantic, Record (a 1970s crisping favourite) and 'the ladies' – Lady Rosetta and Lady Claire, to name a few.

Golden Wonder is perhaps the most famous of this group, bred in early twentieth-century Scotland by Arbroath farmer John Brown when potato 'crossing' was becoming a fashionable pursuit. Golden Wonder, which Brown exhibited at the Smithfield Show in London in 1904, became famous because of its Christmas dinner-worthy quality, dry and firm, happy to be crisped or boiled or roasted. The Scottish crisp company that took its name in 1947 also used the variety to signify the brand's high quality. (Only the name rather than J. Brown's creations remains in the present-day Golden Wonder crisps made by Tayto Group. The company confirmed it's moved on to 'better' crisping varieties.)

And then there's flesh colour. In the case of Walkers, this means a pale yellow crisp that the brand is known for – and which the British crisp-eating population seems to prefer. American consumers like even whiter varieties, which reflects the historical Pacific North-Western potato supply that their chips developed from. In the 1950s, the Lewis Potato Chip Factory in Oregon (tagline: Everybody Eats 'Um, Everybody Likes 'Um) used to give away its browned, rejected crisps for free at the factory door, and I'm sure if I had grown up there and at that time, I would have at least tried them. Detroit's Better Made brand, meanwhile, even has a speciality 'burnt' chip labelled Rainbow, which they have developed expressly for people who miss darker chips.

Potatoes have in-built checks and balances that make it hard to standardise crisps into one international-fits-all product. Pepsi-Co may have its FL 2027 patented potato, which is the classic white base of many Lay's crisps, but it's not like an Apple semiconductor that can be made in Taiwan and shipped in products everywhere. Potatoes need to be grown close to the factory and within the sales territory to make economic sense. The freshest potatoes make the best crisps, and potatoes don't appreciate long-haul journeys, since they are 80 per cent water. Packaged crisps are light but bulky and crushable, and therefore comparatively expensive to shift by freight.

Everything in the crisp world comes back to the parameters of the potatoes, taking leafy instructions from the sun through the stem and translating them underground. You could think of them as at work, in the dark, storing their sugars to feed the potato plants, as stolid in shape as they are in biogenetic purpose. To me, this view makes them mysterious – so sensitive and so vulnerable to forces beyond the grasp of human life. Soil that harbours free-living eelworms, for example, or winds that bring late-blight aphids are enough to ruin a crop completely.

Alternatively, you could see potatoes as something resolutely primeval in plain sight, repeated clearly, telling the same story over again, growing summer after summer, into autumn after autumn, century after century, as above ground the human plot thickens. Stagecoaches turned into bicycles, then cars and crisp-carrying lorries. Perhaps a hundred years from now, drivers will keep crisps in the gloveboxes of flying taxis.

This is one good reason to cherish crisps – for how head-filling and preoccupying they are, a coherent moment noisily stolen in time. Some language on the packet might hint at whether the social norm is to eat this by yourself or share it with others. But in truth, is anyone watching or timing or checking? The crisp eater decides.

If ever you have tended a vegetable patch, and in it grown potatoes, you will know that to stick a digging fork into the earth and hook it upwards brings a marbling of skins through the wet brownness of the soil. And you dig again, in the same spot, and find more. Tinier and ever-tinier little tubers, buried like boiled nest eggs.

When you search for a fact about a potato, the same thing happens. Not one piece of information, but tens, hundreds and then thousands appear in a rubble of facts, because all the facts seem to have relations, contradictory cousins and international counterparts. Potato history is a mess.

Part of the reason for this is that potatoes are asexual breeders. They form themselves from themselves – what is known, horticulturally, as 'vegetatively propagating', which sounds as if they are multiplying in a coma. Fittingly, the shuffling of potatoes around the world began as a casual passing pursuit, far more improvised than designed for its consequences, and therefore patchily recorded.

The awkwardness and the chanciness of our globalised eating are hard to fathom now, since the embeddedness of staple crops in our diet has obscured their geographical origins. But really to describe a history of the potato is to write an inadvertent history of empires and human progress and struggle – of other things that were uneven and unpredictable.

Almost all potatoes emanated from the fecundity of Latin America, the cradle of the Solanaceae nightshade family. There are hundreds of disparate likenesses within this family, genes that link aubergines to petunias and tomatoes to potatoes. When first transported away from their home continent in the sixteenth century, potatoes were passed between conquistadors and dignitaries as small agricultural courtesies, or eaten as ship rations by Spanish soldiers looking for Incan gold. The governor of the Bahamas sent a gift box of potatoes to Virginia in the 1620s, and the crop spread gradually from there through the Northern colonies, although wild potatoes already grew spottily in some North American microclimates.

Meanwhile, potatoes were introduced from Latin America to England and Ireland at some point in the 1580s, although history has a muddled record of whether or not the Spanish, privateers or English aristocratic glory-seekers landed their potato cargo first. The food-loving French novelist Alexandre Dumas père, writing in his *Grand dictionnaire de cuisine* posthumously published in 1873, attributes the honour to Walter Raleigh, and laments that 'This admiral was better known for his enterprising spirit and the vicissitudes of his life than he has been for the importation of the potato.'

The steady illumination of near-equatorial days permits Peru and Bolivia to produce a dazzling multitude of *Solanum tuberosum* varieties from the soil. Originally, these tubers were no bigger than peas or berries, a natural consequence of days that offered roughly the same amount of sunshine throughout the year. Instead of lengthening summer light triggering the tubers to grow bigger, Andean potatoes burst into growth when the days became shorter in the autumn. '*Papas nativas*' are potatoes as European consumers might not recognise them – swollen like fingers with knuckles, their skins and flesh purple or blue or bright yellow. This distinction is celebrated in crisp brands such as Peru's Tiyapuy, which uses high Andean potato varieties and Maras salt, making it probably the most ancestral crisp in the world.

Nikolai Vavilov, a dashing, principled botanist and head of the Lenin Academy of Agricultural Sciences in the inter-war period, called Latin America 'the furnaces of creation', and like his predecessor he made it his mission to learn from the continent to improve Russia's frequently wretched record of agriculture (which had been made even more wretched by Lenin's terrible ideas about collectivised farming).

'We must go to the oldest agricultural countries, where the keys to the understanding of evolution are hidden,' Vavilov declared. He set off in a sequence of often remote expeditions – to Iran, the Pamir Mountains, South America, East Asia – and sent back seed parcels in their thousands.

In a letter to a Russian colleague sent from Peru in 1932, he wrote:

> Studying flowering potato fields in Peru has convinced me that all the so-called local varieties can still be split into hundreds of forms . . . in other words, there are millions of botanical varieties and forms. Our ignorance concerning the Andean potato diversity is striking . . . There is a damned multitude of wild species, but the cultivated potato is such as I have never seen before.

This kind of nationalistically motivated botany was by no means a uniquely Russian pursuit. Spain had collected thousands of Latin American potato samples thanks to the orders of Charles III, who sent botanists Hipólito Ruiz and José Pavón on a ten-year expedition through Peru and Chile in the late eighteenth century. Charles Darwin had brought back a hoard of South American plants on board the *Beagle*, including in 1834 a wild *Solanum tuberosum* specimen from the Chonos archipelago in southern Chile. United States Department of Agriculture professors travelled to Russia in the early twentieth century to collect barley and alfalfa and winter-hardy fruit crops from Siberia.

Wild varieties in Latin America were also found in unusual niches. The Scottish botanist John Maclean wrote in a letter to Sir William Jackson Hooker (then director of Kew Botanic Gardens) in 1849 that he had gathered *Solanum tuberosum* growing in the crevices of rocks in the high-altitude Huamantanga area of Peru.

In southern Chile, the more variable seasons gave the tubers a chance to grow into plumper sizes. Recent analysis by the Natural

History Museum in London and the Max Planck Institute in Germany showed that the commonly chunky white *Solanum tuberosum* that we enjoy today comes from the crossing of Chilean and more northern Andean genotypes taken early on to Europe. (Darwin's Chonos potato was a key piece of evidence in this research.)

Yet in spite of the flurry of cultivar exchanges between nations, the age of mass potato cultivation took time to come about in earnest. There is academic debate about the reasons for this slow start. The food historian Rebecca Earle has argued that far from being mistrusted, the potato was in fact readily accepted and enjoyed by the sixteenth-century European peasantry, who deliberately kept their crops quietly growing in cottage gardens for personal use, to avoid the clerical tithes that applied to crops for sale.

At the same time, there is evidence of the potato struggling with an image problem – what Dumas describes as 'absurd prejudices' that 'prevented [the potato] from being duly appreciated for a long time'. The citations for the potato in Dr Johnson's 1755 *Dictionary of the English Language* are also less than flattering, including these lines by the poet Edmund Waller:

> On choicest melon and sweet grapes they dine,
> And with potatoes fat their wanton swine.

The potato languished in a similar rank to the unloved turnip, which was also pig food, kept away from humans. Russian peasants refused them, although German peasants seemed to plant potatoes without protest. The Danes, in turn, called them 'German lumps'. Danish pastor Lauritz Minis from the island of Funen wrote in his diary at the end of the eighteenth century: 'How to get Potatoes favoured by the farmer is a question of no small difficulty . . . and one could perhaps introduce a new Religion more easily than introduce Potatoes.'

In many European countries, famines were becoming common-place – there simply wasn't enough affordable food for growing populations. In the two hundred years to 1825, the global head-count would double from five hundred million to one billion. Potatoes were a versatile solution, growing in French soil just as readily as they did in fields from Primorye, Russia to Wicklow, Ireland and colonial Calcutta.

In France, the potato had found a cheerleader in the chemist Antoine-Augustin Parmentier. Detained by the Prussians during the Seven Years' War, Parmentier had enough time in jail to notice that he survived well on potatoes and nothing else. Fat-free, gluten-free potatoes and their skins contain good doses of vitamins C and B6, potassium and other nutrients. Once freed from prison, Parmentier began to advocate for potato cultivation in France and later recruited the royal couple, Louis XVI and Marie Antoinette, to his cause. The king and queen wore delicate potato blossoms in their hair and clothes and served potato dishes to their courtiers, attempting to make the *pomme de terre* chic.

During the Paris Commune in the nineteenth century, long after the French royals were guillotined, a section of the Jardins des Tuileries next to the Louvre palace was dug up and replanted with potatoes, Alexandre Dumas notes, earning them the nick-name 'royal oranges'.

Parmentier is honoured in France with a Parisian avenue and an eponymous potato dish – diced cubes wantonly fried in butter, garlic, salt and parsley. The image of him manacled over a bowl of potato-based prison slop is an encapsulation of how potatoes have so often been a route from peril to plenty. But it also expresses how well potatoes can disguise deprivation itself, by being just enough – no more – for survival. American slave narratives, too, feature potatoes heavily as means for subsistence, with some comfort eked out, where possible.

Vincent van Gogh, as a young struggling painter, spent months visiting the cottage of the Groot family in Nuenen, where he lived at the time in the southern Netherlands. Observing as they peeled and cooked and ate the potatoes that they had grown, Van Gogh would come home to make sketches of the memory by lamplight. When in 1885 he produced an oil painting of their dark, cramped evening dinner – potatoes and coffee at 7 p.m. – he wanted it to be daringly true to life: 'something like the colour of a really dusty potato, unpeeled of course'. He succeeded in a dun palette that revealed the family without any trace of pity in the paint. But the frank tone of poverty in *The Potato Eaters* was still met snobbishly by Van Gogh's peers, much to his disappointment.

As millions of breadline families like the Groots grew and subsisted on their own potatoes, the crop began to circulate in a loop of population growth and industrialisation. A break in this loop was devastating enough to have transcontinental consequences – the Irish potato blight in the mid-nineteenth century, for example, not only starved a million people to death, but also forced millions more Irish onto the oceans, seeking better hopes overseas.

This role played by the potato crop means it can act as an early warning signal, even when other means of communication go dark. In North Korea, Kim Jong Un's blackout of information does not extend to his own propaganda, which recently spread the message that potato farming should be encouraged again, as had been the vigorous instruction during the country's famines in the 1990s. This is one of the more public ways in which the country's desperate food shortages become internationally broadcast.

At all points of the globe, in all political scenarios, potatoes and their consumers are vulnerable. Food security acknowledges the presence of risks that transcend state planning and good farming and all the other ways in which we insure ourselves against chaos.

During the siege of Leningrad in the Second World War, the potato curator of the institute of botany dutifully kept the potatoes from deadly frosts by warming a stove with scavenged timber and broken chair legs, at one point tying the seeds up in boxes to save them from starving rats and mice. Most of his colleagues died from starvation at their desks, surrounded by sustenance they had resisted. In a country as beset by crop-savaging storms and bad soil as Russia, a store of this kind was seen to be worth dying for.

Some countries now have a seed bank or seed vault heavily protected from outside forces. Peru's International Potato Center is earthquake-proof. Svalbard Global Seed Vault in Norway is one better, built to survive a hurtling asteroid.

crunch

One evening, around ten years ago, I attended a lecture after work in London given by the Spanish chef Ferran Adrià, of the famed and at that point recently closed El Bulli restaurant, which had gathered three Michelin stars in Roses, Catalonia.

Adrià sprang about the stage in trainers, scribbling professorial and vaguely incomprehensible things on a teacher's whiteboard to explain his theories on the principles of creativity in food. At one point, he stopped. And then he turned and asked the audience if anyone could name the inventor of the omelette. Trick cheffy question. Omelettes, he explained to a room of blank faces, were bound to happen. No one invented them. They invented themselves. Some food is like this. Arguably the best food is like this.

I thought about that evening recently when I revisited Adrià's domestic cookbook, *The Family Meal*, to remind myself of his recipe for a crisp omelette starter, which he pairs with a main course of pork loin with peppers and a dessert of coconut macaroons. Take olive oil, salted potato crisps, eggs, Adrià writes (in so many words). First soak and soften the crisps in the eggs, and then fry the mix into an omelette form, being careful not to break the crisps. No salt – it is already in the crisps.

The result is a shortcut to a light Spanish *tortilla de patatas* – tasty, although hard to eat without feeling some wistfulness that the crisps' crunch has been silenced. To me the crisp omelette was also a revelation – this was not a dish that had come even close to inventing itself in my kitchen before I laid eyes on the recipe, even with my prior crisp obsession, and even with my occasional cooking of a fridge-raiding omelette.

Crisps, on the other hand, seem much closer to Adrià's omelette theory. Somehow, they were bound to happen, or at least that is how it appears now. The very dunness of a potato seems to demand that a transformation or an investigation befalls it, like a lump of clay. More to the point, potatoes call for action to make them edible, similar to other starchy staples such as rice.

The approach to this problem has varied through time. Frozen and dehydrated potato paste, known as *chuño* in Latin America, was the earliest known solution – a way to prolong a source of nutrition when storage was too primitive for the task. In Western Europe, however, it took longer for people to recognise that potatoes could be eaten for joy, and not just for survival. Evidence of potato-joy cooking emerges in records from the eighteenth century, but from well-heeled households who could afford large kitchens and staff.

This bias seemed to hinge on a social paradox – the heavier the weight of potatoes a person consumed in a day, the more they depended on them for life itself, and not for culinary enjoyment. Such was the case in the Great Hunger in Ireland, when kilos' worth of food was fatally withdrawn from the daily diet by the rotted potatoes of the late blight harvest. According to the 1840 Sixth Annual Report of the Poor Law Commissioners for England and Wales, 'labouring poor' men and women in Limerick and Tipperary might have up to four and a half pounds of potatoes in milk for breakfast, the same amount for 'dinner' (lunch) or with herrings if milk was scarce, and possibly no supper at all. Without potatoes, families and communities started dying.

Frivolous, calorific treatments – let alone treats such as crisps – were particularly seen in the kitchens of the upper classes. The Mackenzie family, earls of Seaforth, left behind some extravagant household accounts, now stored in the National Records of Scotland, including bills for twelve hundred champagne bottles from the Edinburgh Glasshouse (1785) and an invoice from Princes Street Coffee House for toasted cheese, lobster, asparagus and spinach and potato salad (1791). This suggests potato was used for nourishing, flavourful cooking in a way that a modern chef might recognise (and great parties, judging by the champagne order).

Again, though there are antiquarian recipe books from the nineteenth century that include crisp-like recipes, they were intended for cooks in 'private families' – those with wealth, status and staff, like the Mackenzies. William Kitchiner, the Jamie Oliver of Regency England, offered one such recipe in his bestselling book *The Cook's Oracle*, published in 1817. 'Peel large potatoes . . . cut them in shavings round and round, as you would peel a lemon; dry them well in a clean cloth, and fry them in lard or dripping,' he advised.

Marie-Antoine Carême, the star chef of nineteenth-century France, wrote an interesting concoction for purple-fleshed *vitelotte* potatoes baked and then doused and mashed with butter, sugar and vanilla-infused milk before being fried into croquettes. Carême suggests adding other flavours – orange and lemon zest, for example. French cookery writer Urbain Dubois also offered in 1890 a recipe for *pommes de terre à la provençale*, which is uncannily like the industrial crisp method – a big vat of olive oil, finely sliced and destarched potatoes, salted and then flavoured with buttered parsley.

In Britain, the crisp had settled into being called a 'game chip', most often served warm with roasted birds such as pheasant or guineafowl. This alliance is not a peculiarly British one, and it lives on in the warmed crinkle-cut crisps that are sometimes served in continental Europe with meat sandwiches and beefburgers. Modern French crisps still carry a serving suggestion on the back packet to heat in the oven *au traditionnel*.

Yet even if the potato was by all accounts no longer shunned, it wasn't yet coveted, either. This shift happened closer to the potato's ancestral home, in the booming Golden Age of East Coast America, in the late nineteenth century. Crisps began to appear there on restaurant menus as 'Saratoga Chips', named for the fashionable Upstate New York resort town Saratoga Springs, where wealthy New Yorkers and other tourists would flock for the summer season.

Saratoga was a place for basking in the sun and in money – playing golf and swimming in the lake or bathing in mineral springs by day, and dining and gambling by night, before retiring to fancy hotel rooms or cottages by the shore, where sail- and steamboats were moored. It was here that crisps first rose to high-fashion status.

The setting was the restaurant at Moon's Lake House, which stood behind a fringe of trees at the head of Saratoga Lake, with a white wraparound porch and always a full dining room. Named for its owner, Mr Cary B. Moon, the establishment was in competition with others set around the shore, and fine dining was an edge. The Grand Union Hotel, for one, had a glitzed dining room fit for an ocean liner.

Moon Lake employed a terrific chef, a biracial Native American–African American called George Crum, whose reputation brought the great and the good to the dining room. According to legend, Crum sliced and deep fried extra-fine wafers of potatoes in response to the requests of a fussy guest, who had ordered crunchy French fries. As local Saratoga historians have pointed out, the story has lots of equivocal places, where 'possibly' prefixes have crept in. The fussy guest was possibly Cornelius Vanderbilt. The real crisp originator was possibly George's sister, 'Aunt Katie', who also worked in the kitchen and may have fried potato rounds by mistake, whereupon her brother may have called it a 'good accident'. The restaurant manager, Hiram S. Thomas, an African American with a fine white wiry moustache, famed for his adroitness and 'celerity' as a head waiter, was also at one point erroneously cited as the potato chip's inventor.

The story nevertheless stuck to Saratoga, and it was a hit. News and approval of potato chips appeared to spread quickly, and 'Moon Brand' Saratoga chips were packaged and sold in souvenir cardboard boxes. A Virginia newsletter, the *Daily Dispatch*, editorialised the potato-chip phenomenon with the statement on 27 July 1878:

> A thing which is of modern origin is the new dish of 'potato chips', which is as far above the Yankee dish of fried potatoes as a sheepshead [fish] is above a mullet. It may seem a small affair,

but I consider it a great one . . . They are excellent and keep well.
They will do to travel on, and are admirable as a breakfast dish.

(Note to self: try crisps for breakfast.)

On 24 August 1878, the *Democratic Advocate* newspaper in
Maryland reported that 'the manufacture of Saratoga fried potatoes, or chips, as they are now called, has become quite a business.
Heretofore this luxury was rarely found outside of a few hotels
and first-class restaurants . . . [Now they] are to be found at all
first-class groceries, and are on the tables at most of the summer
hotels at the mountains and seaside.' The manufacturers preferred
'Jackson whites' for Saratoga chips, the article noted, from the
Idaho potato heartland.

By the 15 August 1880 edition of the *Chicago Daily Tribune*, a
front-page ad for Saratoga Chips declared the product was 'sold
by all the leading grocers' and gave a supply address for hotels and
restaurants at 259 Randolph Street.

If America began its potato-chip story in high places, in Europe,
a democratic, unbranded idea of potato chips gained its first public exposure on the street. London has a long tradition of potatoes
sold as street food, first hawked from barrows pushed by women
and children, as seen in Thomas Rowlandson's 1811 etching of a
female seller shouting, 'Here's your Potatoes four full Pound for
two pence.' Hot potatoes were then sold by at least 1830, according to references in the London Metropolitan Archives.

The middle of the nineteenth century was a turning point
for many industries, as technological progress brought rural

populations to the city seeking work in the factories, often through desperation rather than hope. The 1830s was also the dawn of the age of the public house, another national institution that became in time an accomplice to the British taste for potato crisps.

Steam trains and the arrival of timetabled railways displaced, gradually, the market for bed and board at inns and stagecoaches. Public houses and beer houses (licensed as their names suggest) were places of stopping and drinking and talking, while chains of tearooms took care of more substantial appetites. Locomotive travel sped up the pace and size of city life, and hot potatoes, like crisps, were handy fodder for railway travellers. The 'baked potato man' was a common sight by the end of the First World War, wheeling and stationing a cart around London with warming metal drawers of potatoes and hot spuds ready on spikes.

As was true in the British capital, the streets of Paris were noisy with the cries of different food sellers. A photograph by Eugène Atget taken in 1899 shows a woman selling *pommes de terre frites* on a corner of rue Mouffetard on the Left Bank. Dressed in a white apron over a plain dress, her hands folded primly, she stands by a brazier with a pan on top for frying chips. Small paper bags, napkins and what looks like a salt shaker are ready on a shelf above. A similar set-up is captured in Jean Roubier's photograph of a *pommes frites* seller in Les Halles market in the city centre, taken around 1940, preparing big baskets of chips while women queue up with pails to take them away in.

As the nineteenth century turned into the twentieth, the US was quickly finding an entrepreneurial class, and plenty of small potato-chip companies emerged to take crisps to the retail market. In Cleveland, Ohio, William Tappenden created a crisp factory in his farmyard barn, a kind of crisp side-hustle formula that many other farmers followed. Crisp packages sold in this period for around ten cents apiece – cheap, as crisps always have been, but quick-selling.

The author Mary Antin recalled in her 1912 memoir *The Promised Land* her passage from Polotsk in Eastern Europe to Boston as a child, and her adolescence between two cultures, as America itself shed some of its old ways. From Boston, the Antins moved to the nearby coastal town of Crescent Beach, where her father was to run a beachside tuck shop with his business partner Mr Wilner. They had a busy soda fountain, and sold candy bars and sausages to Atlantic sunbathers, while Mr Wilner took care of kettle-cooking potato chips. Mary adored Mr Wilner, and was transfixed by his potato-chip skill:

Thin as tissue paper, crisp as dry snow, and salt as the sea – such thirst-producing, lemonade-selling, nickel-bringing potato chips only Mr Wilner could make. On holidays, when dozens of family parties came out by every train from town, he could hardly keep up with demand.

The poignancy of Antin's beachside spectacle is partly childhood nostalgia. But to read it now, there is another kind of loss, in the proximity between Mr Wilner and his kettle and the potato-chip customers on the beach. 'In his cook's cap and apron, with a ladle in his hand and a smile on his face, he moved about with the greatest agility, whisking his raw materials out of nowhere, dipping into his bubbling kettle with a flourish, and bringing forth the finished product with a caper.'

I've only seen crisps fried fresh to order outdoors like this once, by a woman in a hairnet making gloriously greasy ready salted in a food truck at a summer fair in Dún Laoghaire, south of Dublin. Since then, I've let the factory-to-fingers distances lapse – I've forgotten about them. There are no more Mr Wilners, just as there is no more Mr Walker. The 'Saratoga' prefix, meanwhile, was dropped from potato-chip packets, quietly. Instead, brands sold their own idea of chips, not a place they came from. Potato chips were everywhere-ness.

The word 'snack', hitherto dormant, rose in usage as the twentieth-century mark passed. From 1900 onwards, it started to climb steeply. Hunger in the new century no longer answered solely to the circadian rhythms of the day. Cities expanded, suburbs sprouted and office buildings filled with workers from the professional classes, who had set their watches by increasingly busy railway timetables. More women were able to join the workforce, and the idea of returning home to eat lunch at the kitchen table faded out. The sale of food was an opportunity in novel niches of the urban landscape, where people hurried, with not much time to linger: the stations, street corners, business districts. Hunger gained a definition by how urgently it should ideally be resolved. Food now had speeds: fast, slow, regular. 'Snack' has its origins in a Middle English word for a dog's snap or bite. To snack is to seize something.

2

a twist of salt

Sometimes – but more often always – on a very long road trip, I will pulverise at least one large bag of crisps. 'To keep me going', as the advice says in my head. With hundreds of miles to cover, usually between Scotland and Wales, even two large bags seem justified. Three is perhaps greedy, but it can be done. (It has been done.)

If well organised, I will buy my car crisps in advance from the Co-op, an insiders' crisp lovers' source that produces the acme of supermarket salt and vinegar, and a good cheese and onion too. Co-op crisps are non-fancy, very crunchy, just-greasy-enough rewards for the scenic never-ending-ness of the M74. Dehydration and a tinge of remorse are worth it. Because as the American author Nathan Sheppard wisely says in his 1887 book *Saratoga Chips and Carlsbad Wafers*, 'The journey is worth all it costs, if it cures you of wanting to be cured.' In other words, there is no better way to get rid of a problem than by forgetting you had it in the first place. Thirst and guilt become more pressing than boredom.

For car crisps, salted flavours are also a logical choice, guaranteed to fire up the neurological pleasure circuits that are dulled behind windscreens and rear-view mirrors. A dose of salt is like blasting the brain with fresh air. Flavourists and crisp-industry insiders call it 'succulence', a feeling of moreish mouthwateringness. It is delightful.

We don't fully know why, however. The mechanisms of salt in the human body are in part mysterious, resembling the swift soar of addiction. A study by Australian scientists at the Florey Institute of Neuroscience and Mental Health found that salt uses opioid signalling in the brain's central amygdala, hitting the high emotional rewards usually reserved for socialising and eating. The pleasure–salt connection, they argued, was a reward for responding to an instinct that aided survival of the species. But if we look closer, we don't fully understand the electrical journey that salt makes to the brain.

We can't resist the salt call. And just as it is a primordial impulse, salt is also an ancient salve. It is an old means for healing and curing, both physiologically and literally, in the case of preserving meats and vegetables. A dose of salt, delivered through a bag of crisps, makes perfect sense as a small luxury, but even more sense as a mini-cure: a short curing of time, a brief curing of hunger, a little curing of distemper.

A literary essayist by trade, Nathan Sheppard was interested in the cult of cures that had lured so many of his fellow so-called 'American dyspeptics' towards Saratoga Springs and Carlsbad in what was then Czechoslovakia, desperate to soothe misunderstood ailments of body and mind by bathing in mineral-spring waters. Like salt, and like potatoes, the spring-bathing cures emanated from the centre of the Earth outwards.

With no little scepticism in *Saratoga Chips and Carlsbad Wafers* Sheppard presented the Milk Cure, the Mugwort Cure, the Shampoo Cure and tens of others – anything that had laid a claim to create some comfort. In spite of the title, little time is given to the solace of potato chips and spa wafers – except, implicitly, Sheppard suggests that their comfort might be as good as any afforded by the Grape Cure, the Swedish Movement Cure or indeed the

Electricity Cure. According to Sheppard's philosophy, if you believe it is working, it is working.

The Winter Cure was one of the oldest of these remedies, a simple swapping of a dull climate for a brighter one, when the coldest months draw in. Crisps and healing here have another twisting of fates. In 1909, an Englishman in Paris, on his way for respite in the Riviera sunshine of Cannes to escape the gas-lit gloom of Edwardian London, inadvertently uncovered a new benefit for Britons: the one I think of today as the Crisps Cure.

In James S. Adam's 1974 book *A Fell Fine Baker: The Story of United Biscuits*, the author recounts the story of this unnamed London produce merchant in 1909 seeing a 'street vendor outside a Paris theatre doing a brisk trade in what he called "perles de Paris"'. The merchant tried the potato wafers fried in 'delectable oil' and was impressed enough to recruit the Parisian crisp vendor and bring him to London two months later in order to develop crisp manufacture at scale.

The produce merchant reputedly went on to work for Meredith & Drew, a London biscuit maker of Victorian vintage that then began to diversify into crisps with a sub-brand called Mandrews Ltd, presumably informed by the Parisian crisp lore of the aforementioned merchant.

At first I admit – perhaps through an entrenched bias about crisps' Britishness – I wondered if this scene of divine Parisian crisp inspiration might be an apocryphal tale. But I found an almost identical account (from which the later version was probably taken) in an unpublished history of Meredith & Drew that appeared in 1950, written by its director and historian, H. Marcus Fisk, contained in the United Biscuits archive.

Swearing to have heard the story first-hand, Fisk (a man apparently known for his 'high principles and wise counsel') elaborated that the London produce merchant was on his way to his winter home in Cannes when he broke the journey in Paris, and went to the theatre one evening. He was 'so struck with the toothsomeness' of the Paris potato pearls that he apprehended the 'bewildered' Frenchman and engaged him to travel to London as soon as possible, unwittingly priming London to scale up an immense British appetite for crisps, from what began as a 'modest basketful' sold to Parisian theatregoers. (I can only imagine the horror of sitting next to someone eating crisps in the fragile dark silence of a theatre.)

It is worth reiterating that by this point America had been stocking its grocery stores with potato chips for at least twenty to thirty years. Many grocers brought in barrels of pay-by-weight crisps fresh from wholesalers, selling them at around twenty-five cents per pound. Brands elbowed into the market and American customers soon had enough pre-packaged choice to begin to pick favourites straight off the shelves: Golden Crisp potato chips versus Ardmore versus Nedo versus Dernell's, taking space alongside other new names such as Kellogg's rice flakes, Sultana Blend coffee, Heinz sweet relish, Campbell's tomato catsup and paper-wrapped Snowflake bread.

In the same period in Britain, there was no record of crisps doing business in this branded way, unlike biscuits, beer, tea and tobacco – particularly biscuits, which were dominated by Huntley & Palmers in Reading, aka 'Biscuit Town'. Captain Scott even took a tin of Huntley & Palmers digestives with him to the Antarctic in 1910, but never opened it. The potato crop yield in America, ironically, was far behind the bushels collected in Europe. But the applications were already commercially more varied, even if the potato industry was worth less than it was overseas.

Yet the drift of food culture, now so powerful from west to east across the Atlantic, seemingly did not translate potato chips into crisps. According to the account of the merchant in Paris, momentum for the British commercialisation of crisps had come from France and not America, a fact that is one of the quieter details in the great British crisp romance.

The outbreak of war in Europe in 1914 marked a significant change in how everyone saw potatoes. In America, President Wilson declared that the nation's greatest responsibility to the war effort for 'the nations' was to create a food surplus at home and to feed Allies overseas. To do so, every American must turn to growing potatoes, he urged. In 1915, the Pennsylvania Railroad Company issued a booklet to help people understand the crop better. 'Every potato produced before next Fall will be more effective, in the cause of the United States and the Allies, than a bullet.'

Propaganda in France, Germany and Britain encouraged people to save bread and eat potatoes, to not waste potato scraps but to meal them into flour, to grow the best seed, to plant more potatoes, to simply think harder about the role of potatoes in staying alive.

'Farmer! Hindenburg calls on you for increased cooperation in the economic battle. This is your patriotic duty just like sacrificing life and limb at the front. Where is the greatest shortage? In cooking potatoes! Germany's potato harvest must never be so low as in 1916,' read one poster. A so-called 'Turnip Winter' followed when the German potato crop faltered. Potatoes became so embedded into the language of wartime that British troops even nicknamed the *Stielhandgranate* (stick hand grenades) thrown by the Germans 'potato mashers'.

When rationing continued in post-First World War Britain, potatoes were among the items approved for unrestricted consumption – last-resort but limitless eating. In this scrappy recovery period, the potato-crisp idea began to rekindle. London grocers started to sell crisps to hotels and pubs, finding mostly male, adult customers and offering only one flavour – plain, with salt shakers used to season at will.

During this nascent period of the crisp market, Carters, a wholesaler in Smithfield in London, recruited Frank Smith, son of a Highgate greengrocer, to become head of its crisp division, selling them in packets. Smith, a hard-working man with slicked-back hair and smart suits, spotted early on that crisp retail could take off in the UK through its then extensive network of pubs, and by adding a crucial ingredient: pre-packaged salt. He believed in the idea so confidently that in 1919, he left Carters and started his own enterprise with a £10,000 capital investment for staff and equipment.

The most reliable account of this story comes from a report in the *Middlesex Independent* of a lecture entitled 'The development of a business' given in 1935 to the Brentford Chamber of Commerce on the 'romance of the crisp' – or how a modern fairytale industry was created from scratch. The lecturer was one Mr Cyril J. Scott, who worked at Smith's as a director.

Scott also credited crisps as a French idea, served in France warm with game as they sometimes were in Britain, he said. Though Carters had been selling crisps since 1913, they were 'not developed' as a product and it took Smith to 'see the possibilities'.

The set-up was an old garage in Cricklewood behind the grand red sandstone frontage of the Cricklewood Crown pub, aided by five tonnes of potatoes, Smith's wife Jessie and a dozen members of staff to help cut the potatoes by hand and carefully shovel the crisps into packets without breaking them apart. Photographs at Brent Archives show a factory floor of primitive efficiency – chutes of crisps like waste flumes heading somewhat unpromisingly towards what look like stainless-steel dustbins.

At the time, this was revolutionary: no one else was manufacturing at the same scale. In the first week, Smith's made 2,646 tins of crisps, and fifteen years later it was firing out 119,000 tins a week. Smith's was not cornering the crisp market, but creating it, and within months Frank, who continued to helm the business after the war, found himself running a national brand. In 1929, it listed on the London Stock Exchange, making it possible to buy and sell shares in crisps (five shillings per share on first issue). By 1934, Scott noted, Smith's had eighty-three farmers in England growing a 'special potato from an imported seed under contract, which showed a profit to the farmers – who had previously got very low prices – and was economic to the firm'. The potatoes were fried in 'finest' Empire groundnut oil.

Switching from horse-and-cart deliveries to motorised transport also improved his service, and Smith's Snackfood Company quickly became the dominant crisp brand in the UK, its delivery vans building valuable sales routes up and down England's arterial roads. Most famously, Smith had added to the greaseproof packets 'a little screw of salt' in a twist of blue paper containing a tiny dusting of seasoning, for the customer to 'shake' to taste.

Scott told his audience that the salt paper might seem like nothing but 'if they ever sent a packet out without it, someone spent a 1½d stamp to write in about it'. (This apparently raised a laugh.) 'Girls had previously been employed to wrap the salt, but now they had 15 machines, each costing £750, to do that job' (some £44,000 per salt-wrapping contraption, in today's money).

Rooting around for the dinky sachet and tearing it open added a layer of ritual to the Smith's brand, leaning into a very British kind of playful habit. The blue salt 'screw' was soon part of the Smith's marketing repertoire, with pin badges and other paraphernalia distributed to its fans.

The unseasoned-to-seasoned flexibility of the Smith's salt twist also made it possible to advertise crisps as an any-occasion snack: the Smith's pony traps were blazoned with the tagline 'Ready for any meal', and early packets elaborated further by declaring the crisps 'Ready for . . . morning bacon, chops & steaks, fish, poultry or game, and cocktails, etc'. The packet also recommends warming the crisps up for two minutes in a hot oven, French-style.

Smith's delivery van slogan was updated by the late 1930s to 'The modern table delicacy', which is similar to how Albert V. Alexander, Labour MP for Hillsborough, described crisps in the House of Commons in a 1936 debate as 'a modern and convenient form of food'. (This is the first mention of crisps in the Hansard records.)

Soon Smith's added a larger factory in Brentford and opened other sites in Portsmouth, Birmingham, Stockport, Lincoln, Paisley, Bristol and Yarmouth. By 1934, Smith's covered 90 per cent of the market with millions of packets sold in Britain that year. The Paige's and Lennard's frying valiantly at Smith's feet had to excel to survive the crunch, but also to get distribution through wholesalers who sold on to publicans and hoteliers. Honourable mention goes to Imperial Crisps Limited, which never even existed, despite trying in 1925 to register a name that all but implied royal assent, a title request that was refused by the Home Office. (We know at least that one royal, Prince Harry, enjoys crisps, from an enthusiastic mention of shopping for them at the supermarket local to Kensington Palace in his memoir *Spare*. Only a handful of crisp brands have royal connections by extension through ownership – United Biscuits, parent of KP Snacks' McCoy's, holds a royal warrant, as does Waitrose, which sells own-brand crisps.)

Scott told the Brentford traders that 'they had had records of 115 competitors since they had started, and now he supposed there were about 15 or 20. They had never attempted to kill competitors by price-cutting or anything like that, but as production had increased they had been able to reduce prices to the retailers and to the wholesalers.'

It was not competition that was the threat in the early days, Scott went on. 'Ridicule had nearly killed the business at first, but that was long past.' Ridicule? I stopped short at this word. Was it really deemed so fanciful that fried potatoes could turn a profit, or was the problem in relation to the lowliness of the potatoes themselves? I could not locate any surrounding sources that would help me to understand the problem, so I'm instead inserting my own, uncertain conclusion: that Smith's crisps were ridiculed simply because the idea was a new one.

Biscuits and cakes, supplied or kept in tins, were already grooved into household shopping lists, and they could be found in the licensed trade, too. But freshly fried potatoes, destined to be eaten as a mouth-watering, 'toothsome' treat as soon as possible, were evidently a harder sell among business peers, in the very earliest days at least.

Crisps in this era came in waxed and stapled glassine packets and had very short shelf lives of just a few days. The American entrepreneur Laura Scudder, who also made peanut butter and mayonnaise, in 1926 pioneered a new kind of sealed crisp packet that meant crisps could enjoy a longer shelf life. Much later, manufacturers introduced the system used today: nitrogen gas blown into cellophane or cellophane–foil hybrids to prolong freshness and protect the crisp curls.

But the perishability of these early crisps didn't matter, because salty potatoes were a thirst maker and salt replacer for pint after pint of beer, plucked out reliably like prizes for all from card-board boxes ranged behind the beer pumps. Crisps have remained a familiar, fond part of British pub culture: a classic meeting of hops and fat, alcohol and salt; an enduringly informal accompaniment to the low-key conversations of pub tables. Crisps, in a loop with booze and socialising, are good for pub cashflow.

This was snack food's first but quiet golden age, and it coincided in Britain with an attempt to remodel the pub itself. In the gin-soaked Victorian age, public houses were ripely all-male enclaves of to-excess alcohol, and though they had shaken off some of the more licentious booziness they still required modernisation.

British pubs had already undergone a strange curtailment in wartime thanks to the government's worries about alcoholism crimping the war effort. Roger Kershaw, at the National Archives, notes that wages had gone up in many heavy industries with over-time hours, which deepened the government's fear that men would simply rush to the pub with wallets flush with cash. To intervene, they enacted state ownership of thousands of pubs in the North and in central Scotland – the so-called Carlisle Experiment – and in 1915 introduced a 'No-Treating Order' that meant you could only buy drinks for yourself and not others. Women and children – and food – were now to be encouraged in pubs, Kershaw added.

The 'improved pub' movement after the war saw big breweries forking out much of the cash needed to smarten up their tied premises. Some built new pubs from the ground up on middle-class estates, such as the Windermere in South Kenton, which was constructed by Courage Brewery and is still in use today (now serving Tayto crisps from behind the bar).

Inter-war British pubs were designed and remodelled with the express purpose of emerging as respectable places for women and families to pass time – largely thanks to the introduction of open-plan rooms and the removal of drinking partitions. 'Road-houses' became popular for the new motoring classes. Crisps were part of the democratisation of pubs as national living rooms, symbolising the good things – the small treats – one could expect from them. In some villages without a corner shop the pub would even double as a mini grocery store, selling dry goods such as sweets and crisps over the bar. Children could also be seen waiting outside pubs in the hope that an adult would relent and buy them a packet.

Before it was culturally commonplace for women to be at the bar, men got the lion's share of crisps, which were mostly sold in the hospitality trade until the 1960s. The connection between crisps and gender crossed my mind when reading the short story 'The Man Who Ate Spain', by Irish author Cróna Gallagher. In it, Gallagher imagines the life of a man who eats only crisps, from boyhood to manhood – a life of some difficulty socially, alongside the freedom that comes with sticking to one idea. She shows, with nicely acid humour, the twin absurdity and validity of his attachment, which I acknowledge in mine.

Johann Sebastian, the anti-hero of the story, thinks of 'cheese "n" onion' and 'salt and vinegar' as the Adam and Eve of the potato-crisp world. 'But which was male and which was female?' The notion of the 'manliness' of crisps is meanwhile comically explicit in a newsreel from 1957, which documented the competitive-eating exploits of the Northumbrian miner Joe Steel. The tape begins as Joe is coming off shift at Choppington Colliery, dressed down in cloth cap and jacket, coal soot still smudged on his face. 'Joe Steel does a man's job underground. He believes in spending his leisure in a man-sized way as well,' the reel's narrator tells us. To pursue man-sized leisure, he heads for his local pub, the Howard Arms in Bedlington, where he was 'a well-known regular, particularly well known to landlord Crinian'. Joe has a parlour trick, the narrator explains, which brings in customers from 'far and wide'. This trick is to eat huge quantities of crisps at speed, measuring himself against the clock.

Joe Steel is Britain's 'champion potato-crisp eater', we learn. 'His undisputed record, set up last Easter Monday, is thirty-five packets in forty-five minutes.' This spectacle – Joe on a crisp tear, assisted only by his 'second in command', who opened the packets for him – was apparently good business for the Howard Arms. 'Joe Steel in action is a sight to astound any casual visitors who don't know what's going on.'

In the past, we learn, Joe has also eaten record quantities of sausages and black pudding. The camera observes as he ploughs crisps into his mouth, where they vanish. Fifty minutes is rung on the bell. 'This time Joe's score was thirty-five packets of crisps.' Not quite a personal best. He ends the session nonetheless with a celebratory yard of ale. Pub, crisps, beer – a classic trio of baseline masculinity, supersized to absurd proportions.

More substantial pub food didn't emerge until the 1960s, giving crisps a long run, broken by the Second World War, of featuring on a very short list of things to eat at the bar. And it was the salt that kept them there: the refreshing, dehydrating, refreshing, dehydrating loop that is the booze-and-crisps winning circular formula. Wherever you buy crisps, alcohol will be beside or behind you, and vice versa: wherever you buy alcohol, a hedge of crisps will be growing close by, flourishing to shoulder height. An arm's reach is all it takes. Wine and crisps: a double cure.

Ever since salt progressed from its older role as a curer and preserver of food, humans have arranged much of our eating around it, and used proximity to salt as an incentive in forming new settlements, such as Salzburg or Saltcoats. Salt is valuable enough to have been used as a prompt for taxes in colonial India and as a form of salary in the Roman army, when it was boiled from seawater in evaporating furnaces, or taken where possible from salt springs. In a 1921 essay on the symbolic significance of salt, the psychoanalyst Ernest Jones noted that 'in Ancient Rome soldiers and officials were paid in salt instead of money, whence (from salarium) the modern words "salair" and "salary" and the phrase "to be worth one's salt" (to be capable, to earn one's salary)'.

Jones's essay is a probe into the reasons for salt's pervasive presence in folklore, religion and superstition, prompted by the notion that it is bad luck to spill table salt. 'In all ages salt has been invested with a significance far exceeding that inherent in its natural properties,' he writes, going on to explore quirks of salt's meaning in different cultural circumstances. It can preserve from decay or remove the sins of the dead, and is disliked by the devil or is good luck for newlyweds, depending on where you pin the map.

> Where in one country the presence of salt is indispensable, in another one abstinence from salt and at the same time from sexual intercourse is equally essential. Both cases agree in regarding salt as an important agent in these respects; whether this is for good or for evil is of secondary interest, the main point being its significance.

Salt has loomed symbolically large in the crisp industry, too, on both sides of the bargain. It is the fundamental seasoning common to almost all brands, a kind of god of all crisps, and it is also the shopper's shorthand for a massive array of different products, grouped together in the universal language of 'salty snacks'.

But salt is now at a point where its fundamental presence in the product is no longer so desirable, given the health implications of a high-sodium diet. Food businesses are all undertaking, with varying degrees of enthusiasm, programmes to reduce the salt content of their products. Some brands already sell crisps completely undressed, with no flavouring at all, such as Tyrrells Naked – a move that is both retro, recalling Smith's undressed – and modern, evoking health.

I met Matthew Bailey, professor of renal physiology at Edinburgh University's Centre for Cardiovascular Science, at Press Cafe on Buccleuch Street in the Scottish capital, a tiny, navy-painted coffee house that looks on to quiet passing scenes near the faculty. Our discussion was about his speciality – the effect of salt on health – but as an ice-breaker I was somewhat relieved to hear that he is partial to salt and vinegar crisps.

'Salt is such a societal, integral part of human fabric,' he said. 'This relationship with salt was originally driven by a physiological need, then it became synonymous with economies. Relatively recently it's become a widespread commodity locked in foods that we probably don't really think about.'

Unlike sugar, salt isn't a nutritional indulgence or luxury. Without some salt in their diet, humans would die, because 'everything needs body salts', Bailey said, to maintain cellular health. Our urge for salt is not the same as greed.

Before our diets became industrialised and packaged goods became widespread, most salt in Western diets came from meat, a handful of plants and mined mineral salts. Salt was a cooking 'spice' in medieval times, but it was far less readily available than pepper, and most commonly used to preserve fish and meat through the winter. Sugar became fashionable and coveted long before salt did.

'Our estimates are that we need half a gram a day, give or take. And the World Health Organization recommends no more than five grams a day,' Bailey said, sipping a latte. 'That's not a recommended amount, but an upper limit tolerable for health.'

In the UK, the recommended upper limit is six grams. 'But globally, humans eat between eight and twelve grams a day. We're eating twenty times what we need physiologically.' Most people are 'wildly inaccurate', Bailey says, about how much salt they eat. If you measure out a gram of salt on an electric scale, it looks like a spilled trail from a cooking spoon. It is barely enough to season a soup. Bailey mentions a salt-reduction programme conducted by the Chinese government in 2007 by issuing five million plastic measuring spoons to urban households, so that they could limit themselves to one salt scoop a day. Even in a society with less than democratic political systems, mass changes to diet still have to be voluntary.

Bailey conducted an experiment on himself in which he and his colleagues tested his own blood for salt levels after a day of regular eating. He estimated the result would be well below the recommended amount, but in fact it was eight grams. Some of his colleagues managed to get their salt below five grams a day, but only through a comically laboured programme of spartan self-control.

This might not be a problem, but for the fact that our ignorance of our true salt intake is mirrored in our ignorance of our blood pressure levels, an unfortunate combination given that high salt intake is linked to high blood pressure.

We adapt to high sodium by taking on more water so that 'the internal sea is kept at the right amount'. This leads to the 'pressure going up in the tank'. There is an intimate relationship between salt and water. Thirst and salt go in different pathways in the brain, but they 'talk to each other'.

The best thing you can do is reduce salt as much as possible, although this is inevitably a process of acclimatisation, rather than sudden severance.

'When you try to walk away to a lower-salt food it tastes very bland. It takes between two and six weeks to readjust to a lower salt level. But you can tolerate low amounts of salt.'

For context, in a single forty-gram packet of Walkers Thai sweet chilli crisps, there is 0.32 grams of salt. This is a pretty standard amount across most crisp manufacturers, and Walkers, like other brands, have active salt-reduction programmes.

All this is complicated by the fact that the amount of time it would take someone to adjust to a low-salt diet is not standard across a population. It is specifically related to their salt sensitivity, which is to say that not everyone tastes salt the same way.

'There are studies a hundred years back looking at salt and blood pressure, and even then you can see some people could eat quite a lot of salt and be fine and others would become ill – those are the salt sensitive, the ones we'd have to worry about. But I believe that everyone's health is adversely affected by high salt intake, with the exception of rare disorders where you can't hold on to salt.'

The 'salt sensitive' represent around 30 per cent of people, a 'large minority' versus the 'salt resistant'.

In relation to crisps, salt is one of the few flavourings that is 'open-market' – its formula is not proprietary or exclusive to any one manufacturer. Every consumer knows what salt tastes like. Surprise and novelty come from pairings such Kent Crisps' sea salt and oyster crisps, or recondite provenances, such as the Peruvian Maras salts with *papas nativas*. Not all salts are created equal, either. My preference is for the more obviously salted numbers such as Kettle Chips, which even in their lightly salted flavour don't disguise the presence of oil and large salt crystals.

The challenge that all manufacturers face is how to reduce salt: as an inescapable part of healthy eating consciousness, it is what the consumer wants to see, but achieving it is a matter of complexity for the crispers.

Unlike sugar, salt is inimitable. It can't be easily substituted. In general cookery there are sugar-adjacent flavours that could enhance the impression of sweetness in a dish. But the translation doesn't work for salt. It's a little ironic in a category that thrives on imitation: powdered flavouring can dress a potato as almost anything else from a doner kebab to a garlic prawn or sriracha mayonnaise, but the emulation of salt itself is elusive.

In the broader realms of industrial science, some attempts are already being made at a different route around the problem. Instead of reducing salt, the thinking goes, why not try to make salt itself taste saltier?

Chromovert, a technology patented in 2022 by a biotech start-up based in the United Arab Emirates, Secondcell Bio, scans millions of cells to pinpoint those with very specific agencies. In its own words, this is 'cell engineering technology to detect and purify living cells based on expression of one or more sequences of interest'. The relevant patent statement confirms that an application of the technology was 'assessed and confirmed in human sensory studies to enhance the salty taste of sodium chloride'. The company is not currently affiliated with any crisp manufacturer.

But the precedent could point to a possible diffusion of this kind of technology into mainstream food products, a way perhaps of using less salt without compromising on salt taste.

MicroSalt, an American company that specialises in low-sodium snacks, also has a SaltMe! potato-crisp brand that uses a patented salt to deliver 'natural salt with approximately 50 per cent less sodium'. The company says the salt 'dissolves immediately when it touches your taste buds, delivering a more intense taste of salt'.

As discussed previously, the seemingly harmless, even beneficial deception – less salt for the same taste – can only operate in conjunction with the mouth and the brain, which control our sensory perception.

Stephen Roper, a professor in the Department of Physiology and Biophysics at the University of Miami's Miller Medical School, spoke with me via Zoom in the middle of his day of consultations and supervision of medical students. (One of them knocked on the door, at one point, to politely declare that a patient didn't look too well.)

Roper is interested in how the brain comes to understand the saltiness of salt through the taste buds. In a paper he wrote: 'As few as three decades ago, taste buds were merely considered inactive interfaces between flavorsome chemicals in the oral cavity and interpretive centers in the nervous system.'

This perception has now been proved to be incorrect. Taste buds don't simply pass on information, but sort it and shape it too. 'We now understand that the taste bud is a community of interacting cells with significant cell–cell communication taking place during gustatory excitation. Taste buds are no longer thought of as passive sensory structures.' When salt is on our tongue, one of two things happens: the level is deemed either preferable (salted crisps, for example), or aversive (a gulp of seawater), and two different mechanisms send this information on separate pathways.

Work by others, including Akiyuki Taruno at Kyoto Prefectural University of Medicine in Japan, has identified some of the cell types in the taste buds that sort different tastants such as salt, but there is 'still some ambiguity about those that respond to sodium', Roper said. The mystery starts to deepen when scientists try to understand how 'salt is converted into an electrical signal and transmitted to the brain', Roper told me.

He parses it in technological terms: 'Our taste buds are like little microcomputers; we know what the input is, we're trying to work out how that correlates with the output.' He describes this as 'a discussion' between the cells in the taste bud, as if to say, 'OK, a little bit of sodium has come in,' and then a synaptic interaction follows. 'Lord knows what it is,' he added. 'It's sorting a salad of signals. You can manipulate the circuitry, but it's at the edge of research, and these interactions we see independently in a microscope we can't see in an intact person.'

Temperature and fatty content and texture are analysed in the brain, and detected more quickly than satiation, which can take 'minutes to hours'. Unfortunately, if you're like me, you continue to enjoy fatty content and salty texture freely, and fail to stop when common sense instructs you to. I need more than the signal from the rational, unsalted part of my brain.

I can happily drive from one end of the country to the other without obeying a single traffic light for salt. I like being cured of the need to be cured.

3

humble beginnings

A June night, 1943. Flight Lieutenant George Duffee lowered his feet into the dark. Below him – he didn't know exactly where – lay the border between Germany and the Netherlands. Luftwaffe night fighters had picked off his sortie on the return to Bomber Command, and the rest of his Halifax aircrew were dead in their seats. All he could do was parachute down as the plane fell, into either enemy or occupied territory.

Duffee jumped. When he landed, safely, the white silk canopy collapsed behind him against something rumpled: a potato field. 'I could feel the potatoes,' he remembered, decades later.

While he got to his feet, people began to gather at the edges of the field. The first person who spoke to him was a man wearing a pair of clogs. A farmer. Duffee was safe enough, for now, on Dutch potato land. He asked if he could borrow the farmer's shoes, instead of wearing his 'dead giveaway' flying boots, to which the man eventually agreed, also giving him a change of clothes. 'I buried the parachute, and made good my exit,' he said. He threw the boots into a hedge. Months later Duffee had managed to reach Gibraltar via the so-called Comet Line, smuggled through a Resistance network from Brussels to Paris and on to the Pyrenees and Spain. He arrived back in Britain in September 1943, when the Dutch farmer would have been thinking about his harvest.

Another global conflict had brought potatoes into the fight. To join an army in the Second World War was to broach the chance of killing and dying, but most recruits had to suffer the drudge of peeling potatoes, too. Soldiering was getting by, and surviving on spuds and tinned protein was a chore shared by most forces, regardless of their uniform. Crop sabotage and theft were commonplace.

Potato memories, so often life or death in tone, stayed with the survivors. A French Resistance fighter remembered desperately picking off Colorado beetles from the few potato plants that grew in her garden. It was all she had to eat. A US Army Air Force pilot remembered leaving New York Harbor in 1942 on board the SS *Pasteur*, a French liner converted for troop movements, and discovering its on-board swimming pool drained of water and filled instead with potatoes. They were everywhere.

War had been a boon for British spuds. Two-thirds of Britain's food prior to 1939 was imported, and to feed a nation now recruited to one purpose, total war, 'something had to be done', as a Ministry of Information cinema reel recalled in 1946. To boost home supplies and compensate for the blockage of imported goods, the Ministry of Food instigated a massive programme of agricultural investment, throwing £100 million at new equipment, and turning over six million acres of grasslands to wheat and vegetable production. 'Our very soil was conscripted,' the MoI reel narrator relates sombrely, as civilians are shown digging up golf courses. Temporary laws were even drafted to permit the labour of schoolchildren at potato harvest. (They had to be twelve years or older, and were paid for their efforts at specially organised 'harvest camps'.)

The Ministry of Food's Advice Bureau got behind the potato as an appetising thing to eat with a publicity drive featuring a cartoon character, Potato Pete, recruiting home cooks to his recipes for champ, scalloped potatoes and potato fingers. Potato Pete had a sidekick named Dr Carrot, who gamely wore a top hat and jaunty spats over his shoes.

Yet in reality most of what wartime Britain ate was preordained by 'diet sheets' and fixed prices and state-subsidised restaurant menus. Community schemes such as Pig Clubs, whereby a handful of locals would share their time and household waste to care for and fatten small pigs, doubled the chance that you were eating exactly the same dinner as your neighbours. Village Produce Associations, meanwhile, made use of surplus fruit and vegetables, so that a rural grocer might sell American dried milk alongside blackberry jam from a nearby hedgerow. Allotments grew bushily in number and were actively encouraged.

Peacetime meant prolonged rationing, and yet more potatoes. The Agriculture Act of 1947 brought in by the new Labour government was designed to help farming and associated industries such as the crispers get back to business, by guaranteeing prices for staple crops. Potatoes were effectively state-subsidised, with conditions wrangled by the Potato Marketing Board, which liaised with farmers and potato merchants on land use and regulations.

The continuous factory production of wartime meant that brands that had adjusted commercial operations were in theory poised to resume full-throttle business as usual. But it wasn't always so simple. Meredith & Drew's main factory at Shadwell in East London near the docks was destroyed in 1940 during the Blitz, and crisp operations were temporarily moved to the old

Betta Biscuit factory nearby, while a new dedicated crisp plant opened at Woodville, near M&D's wartime HQ at Ashby-de-la-Zouch. Energy supply in wartime was mainly syphoned towards munitions, meaning some factories in strategic regions found their power cut off completely. There was also a shortage of 'soft oil' in which to fry the potato slices, which limited production scale.

As soon as the war ended, the dominant player, Smith's, made immediate plans to increase production capacity. The firm had continued to perform well during wartime – at its 1941 annual general meeting, Smith's chairman Sir Herbert K. E. Morgan noted proudly that turnover had held steady for the second year running. 'As in times of peace our crisps have been a standby, and an always reliable friend – they are additionally so these days.' Morgan added that crisps were in high demand from troops on active service, and were a good 'emergency food' that could be taken without fuss to air raid shelters. No cooking needed, and no risk of spoiling (in theory). But throughout the war, Smith's had been unable to keep up with demand: its supply chains were fractured by the conflict, and shopkeepers would frequently have to turn away customers asking for crisps, Morgan said.

Not long into peacetime, a new art deco-style Smith's factory was operational in Fforestfach, northern Swansea, bringing to eleven the total number of factories run by Smith's, alongside twelve depots. When Morgan addressed the Smith's AGM in 1949, he declared that the company now employed more than two thousand people, having started in 1920 with just a dozen staff. Crisps created jobs that had never been done before.

humble beginnings

Seaman Tom Barker came home from the war in 1946 with a demobilisation stipend of £68 (about £2,300 today), and two 'terrible suits' offered free by the navy to dress for life on civvy street. He had served aboard HMS *Duff* and HMS *Victorious*, and arrived back with a thud in Darlington, County Durham, where he found work in an aluminium factory making cooking pans. And then he saw a newspaper ad for a better job: driver-salesman for Smith's potato crisps.

'There was only one firm on the go at the time,' he recalled, 'and that was Smith's.'

Barker couldn't drive – so in order to sell crisps, he had to get his driving licence first, and then report for duty. He duly turned up with his piece of paper at the Smith's office in Richmond Castle, and was introduced to someone he already knew. Surprise of the day, he thought. Then he was shown to his company car, which turned out to be a 1932 Rolls-Royce. 'They said, "There's your car." Pea green, twenty-one-inch wheels, eight mile to the gallon,' he recalled fondly. 'I used to go up and down the Dales [in the Rolls-Royce] selling crisps. I became pretty well known.'

Baker was paid £7 (about £240 today) a week for his crisp chauffeuring – really 'not much money' for a full-time job. But he remembered enjoying the work, and bartering crisps with other local traders for bread and beer. 'Them days, it was all "swap this and swap that".' Van sellers were a regular feature of most retail – there was one for bread, another for fish, and they would turn up at roughly the same time each week, an anticipated part of the community routine.

The idea of a network of driver-salesmen was important to crisps in Britain, just as it would prove to be for potato chips and snacks in America. As Baker spun around the Dales in his pea-green Roller, Herman Lay had already spent years on the road as a route salesman in Nashville, selling Lay's potato chips from the boot of his Model T Ford.

Motorised transport was instrumental in expanding the market for crisps, but it also relieved the problem of time fighting against freshness of the product. Lorries, rather than cars, were needed to take potatoes in bulk from the field to the factory and tins of products on to the shops, pulling off an early version of 'just in time' logistics. Road freight also required fast roads, of which Britain had none after the war. The M1 did not open until 1959, and even then it only stretched from Watford to Northamptonshire, at the foot of the new crisps country forged in Leicester by Henry Walker in 1948. Eventually the M1 linked up to the A1, which reached Edinburgh, where William Alexander had started Golden Wonder in 1947.

These two companies, the UK's leading twentieth-century crispers alongside Smith's, both started in the ashes of war. Walkers Crisps was a rescue mission to prop up Henry Walker's main business, a pork butcher's shop, which had floundered with the strictures of meat rationing. William Alexander, who mended televisions and radios by night for extra cash, used the doughnut fryer at his bakery to make his first batches of Golden Wonder crisps, sold hot from the oven like bread rolls. His granddaughter, Jennifer Fraser, later recalled a childhood trip to the Golden

Wonder factory in Sighthill, Edinburgh with her grandfather, and the joy of being given a bag of crisps straight from the production line: 'The smell of salted crisps was amazing . . . They are lovely when they are still hot.'

Both Walkers and Golden Wonder quickly found favour, but they remained regional, family affairs, born on the high street. Britain's post-war economy, too, was still reorienting itself. In 1953, the minister of food, Major Gwilym Lloyd George, agreed to change rationed allocations for the queen's coronation so that street-party tables would not go empty, and expected flocks of tourists could be served complete hot breakfasts. 'There will also be provided small quantities of sugar or fat needed to increase supplies of other items,' he told Parliament, 'such as potato crisps, toffee apples, popcorn and candy floss which are so popular with children.'

(Contrast this with the carefree portrait of gleeful crisp eating in the American jazz singer Slim Gaillard's 1952 hit, 'Potatoe Chips' – a song written by Gladys Carr and Julia Bunora about the irresistibility of crunchy chips, and the availability that went along with the taste; there's always a 'bag around', the song says.)

By the middle of the 1950s, when British rationing had been fully lifted, the volume of potatoes farmed for the express purpose of being turned into crisps had reached 50,000 tonnes, according to the Potato Marketing Board's newsletter, *Potato Post*. That rose to 320,000 tonnes by 1966, and 535,000 tonnes by 1970. The Potato Marketing Board started to draw up template contracts for farmers to use when beginning negotiations with the crispers. They urged, in the *Potato Post*, that farmers should take the crisping opportunity seriously.

Around the same time, the experience and culture of food shopping in Britain were themselves undergoing a revolution. Half a million British women had been drafted into military service during the war, and 2.5 million more into the factories, some into 'shadow' factories hidden in the countryside from Luftwaffe target maps. Others 'dug for victory' in the Women's Land Army. When war ended, women were urged to find work in industries once more, to help fix a now acute labour shortage, but the old norms of housewife at home, man at work were frustratingly obstinate.

Food – buying and cooking it – was an expected consumer of women's time and an implicit interference with their professional freedom. To stand in a queue at the grocer's, and wait for the goods to be picked off shelves, and wait for food to be weighed, and wait again to pay all added up to a valuable portion of the day. While chains of grocery stores had emerged in the early twentieth century with Waitrose, Tesco and J. Sainsbury's, they had no connection to speed and convenience.

Instead, they followed the weigh-and-serve traditional counter-service model, which was a cumbersome ritual of wait-your-turn and what-can-I-get-you. In 1948, the Co-op tried something different. On Ipswich High Street, it opened its first – and the nation's first – permanent self-service store, inspired by the model that had already taken off in America, where labour shortages during the war had propelled the idea into action. Tesco's founder Jack Cohen also travelled to America after the war and saw a vision of food retail that he brought back to the UK, with his own debut self-service Tesco store also unveiled in 1948. The Co-op added hundreds of other self-service supermarkets in the 1950s, and others followed suit, with patchy results.

The modestly sized grocery store, wedged firmly on the high street, remained the norm until later in the 1950s, when fuel and construction limits were finally unbound. More Britons than ever were now living in flats, and fewer and fewer people employed household staff. Prepared foods were therefore in demand. At Smith's AGM in 1950, Herbert Morgan noted that 'Crisps can be eaten hot or cold, and served with any meal, saving trouble and labour to the housewife'. He was also keen to persuade shareholders of subtler shifts in society that would aid the cause of crisps, including the fact that more people were spending time outdoors, he said – going to the beach, for example, and arranging picnics. Britain was loosening up, and it needed more snacks. (With the possible exception of the poet T. S. Eliot, whose character Julia in the 1950 play *The Cocktail Party* declared: 'Potato crisps? No, I can't endure them.')

By 1954, the American self-service Safeway chain began scoping the possibility of an English expansion, spurred on by the experiments of Sainsbury's, Home and Colonial Group and the International Tea Company. 'Help yourself' was the new protocol for buying food. Choose what you want, when you want, and in whatever quantity.

Some viewed this wanton basket-filling with suspicion.

crunch

Even as late as 1980, an employee wrote to Sainsbury's in-house staff magazine, *JS Journal*, with misgivings about a shopper's behaviour.

From: Derek Wood, Blackfriars

In my local Sainsbury's I saw a woman eating from a packet of Sainsbury's crisps while doing her shopping. At the time I saw her the packet was nearly empty and she was some distance from a checkout. Is this a new form of shoplifting?

The editor of the magazine replied:

In the trade this kind of behaviour is called 'grazing'. Most 'grazers' produce the empty packaging at the checkouts and pay in the normal way but as you suggest some people do see it as a way of getting a free meal. We hope to look at this and other aspects of shoplifting and dishonesty in greater depth some time later in the year.

Grazing, visually at least, began a conversation between the customer and the product, without an interlocutor. An opportunity emerged for brands to speak in this language, to find catchphrases that suited the national mood. Even the most famous political statement of the 1950s, prime minister Harold Macmillan's 1957 declaration that most people 'have never had it so good', sounded like it could be printed on to a packet of soap flakes.

humble beginnings

In Italy, a tiny grocery store opened in 1936 in a Milan side street, named after the nearby church of San Carlo al Lazzaretto. It started its potato-chip sideline by delivering crisps to bars and bakeries by hand. Then it moved to delivery by bikes, and then, as the order sheet grew longer, Fiat Topolinos. Now San Carlo potato chips is owned by Migros Group, and turns over tens of millions of euros. This basic logic applied everywhere: businesses needed roads and railways to become empires (as well as good management and good products).

The significant head-start that Smith's had on all crisp speculators in post-war Britain did not prevent it, in a matter of decades, from making mistakes that would eventually lead to its decline and sale in the late 1960s.

Nothing in its 1950s organisation foretold this struggle, not least its superbly efficient delivery system. In an article on Smith's Crisps published in August 1951 by *Commercial Motor* magazine, journalist Alfred Woolf described how crisps used to be a 'seasonal delicacy, like oysters', because of the problem of not being able to get potatoes into production fast enough.

'To-day, fresh crisps are available in every town and village in the country,' Woolf went on. 'At present, rationing of the special edible oil in which the crisps are cooked restricts output, but even so, over 5m. bags of crisps are sold weekly. Each year, over 30,000 tonnes of potatoes are needed to meet the demand.'

Woolf inspected Smith's estate at Nocton, near Lincoln, which churned out ten thousand tons of potatoes for its factories every year. He was starstruck, as a motoring journalist might be, by the estate fleet of long-wheelbase lorries, tractor-drawn trailers, tippers, Morris and Albion delivery vans and even a light railway that could carry ten tonnes of spuds to nearby factories. The Albions could accommodate two thousand tins of crisps, some of them strapped to the roof racks if required. (The tins were collected and reused as part of the delivery routine.)

Cyril J. Scott, director of Smith's transport system, who had served as a sergeant during the war, said to Woolf of the driver-salesmen that they were 'entrusted with the duty of obtaining orders as well as of delivering them. Customers have been known to set their clocks by the arrival times of these drivers.'

For a different reason, the critical business burden of the transport systems was also pinpointed by Mr Fisk in his history of Meredith & Drew. He lamented the 'disproportionate amount of transport required to carry crisps as against that for biscuits'. Crisps were light and took up space, so:

> a lorry load of biscuits might contain say two tons worth £100 [but] the same lorry loaded with crisps might not contain more than half a ton [with a] value, of course[,] even proportionately less. This has indeed been the rock upon which has split practically every manufacturer who has ever set up the production of potato crisps . . . The moment he begins delivery even for a mile or two the oncost amounts to more than the actual intrinsic value of the article itself.

The lure of ready-worn sales routes and factory sites was a pressing motive for crisp businesses to start buying one another.

humble beginnings

When the Frito Company, a San Antonio, Texas corn-chip maker, was merged in 1961 with H. W. Lay & Company, based in Atlanta, Georgia, potato and corn power were now linked up coast to coast with factories, sales territories, brands and employee knowhow. 'No other company in the industry is so equipped nationally,' Frito-Lay's annual report proclaimed in 1961, and it was right.

Frito-Lay was ready to exploit a distribution network as thorough and strategic as an army with military bases, counting forty-eight manufacturing plants in total. The merged operation also boasted 2,800 driver-salesmen, who acted as store-to-store sales reps and truck-delivery men.

Even before the merger, the Frito Company was exceptionally well run. Its sales routes had begun in late 1930s South-Western and Western states before pushing into the Great Lakes and the East Coast, producing Fritos, Ta-tos and Cheetos to the 'whopping total' of almost 190 million packets in 1953 alone.

Each Frito division had clear corporate goggles on: Dallas was for engineering excellence, making new equipment and sales racks, while Denver handled potatoes through a specialist subsidiary for Ta-tos. Every single plant, from Amarillo to Salt Lake City, churned out the bestselling Fritos, to keep up with consumer demand. Highly refined vegetable oil usage in the Frito Company 'hit the 7,916,847 pound mark, which is equivalent to 132 railroad tank cars', the annual report for 1953 notes. The company's legal department turned out to be operationally vital, snuffing out the many competitors who snuck onto the market with uncannily Frito-esque branding.

The consolidated corn-to-potato snack empire (which also subsumed Frito's and Lay's respective hordes of sub-brands such as Ruffles potato chips, Baken-ets fried pork rinds and Rold Gold pretzels) is politely bullish in its first annual report, talking of 'progress' that brought about in excess of $127 million in sales – about $1.4 billion in today's money.

The new enlarged company, based in Dallas, also had Lay's distribution in the South-East to join up with, in many cases continuing franchisee arrangements already in place between Frito and Lay's for the latter to sell the former's products. Noting the possibility for new sales opportunities with its now national snack reach, it promised an 'aggressive' marketing campaign. 'It will be the company's dedicated purpose for the next few years to create greater consumer preference for all of its products throughout the United States.'

This was a critical moment in the cultural realm of snacks. A Russian doll effect of ownership has since become commonplace, with one company subsuming another, and the parent doll becoming ever larger – as if, like the crisp eater, the eyes must always have an appetite greater than the stomach. It is a principle that has instituted so much complex change beyond the boundaries of a crisp factory: for if brands become national, and therefore nationally cherished, they create a certain amount of capitalistic headway. But the cherishing of individual brands and products feels more personal to the end buyer, introducing a disjointed attachment between the brand, the maker and the consumer's loyalty. We're used to product packets having two sides

– the face, with branding, and verso, with small print detailing a contract of modern living that we won't read. A merger of the scale of Frito-Lay introduced a third kind of invisible contract, in which the consistency and pervasiveness of the product is taken on trust to mean that the complexity behind the scenes is not worth thinking about.

Internally, Frito-Lay credited its employees for its success, coming as they did from companies of 'humble beginnings' in the grip of America's Great Depression. Frito Co. was started by Charles Elmer Doolin in 1932 with a potato ricer and a recipe for fried corn chips that he had bought for $100 ($75 of which was a loan) from a cafe owner in San Antonio, who reputedly wanted the money so they could return to Mexico. Doolin made the first batches of his corn chips in his mother's kitchen, and was relentlessly resourceful and shrewd. By the time he died of a heart attack in 1959, just before the merger, Doolin was chair of the board of a company employing 3,500 people across America, with $51 million in annual sales. After the amalgamation with Lay's, there was no trace left of modest beginnings. Frito-Lay had America's appetite at its feet.

Across the pond, in 1960, Golden Wonder had begun to produce ready salted crisps in which the salt was already shaken inside, as if the sachets had vanished into thin air. The following year, the crisp company that began as a tiny Edinburgh bakery was sold to a new owner. It had caught the eye of a completely different industry, far outside the food world. Imperial Tobacco, then Britain's largest nicotine brand selling cigarettes and pipe tobacco including Capstan and Player's Navy Cut, now had a share in crisps, for a purchase price of £490,000 (about £9 million in today's money).

Imperial Tobacco had recovered almost 100 per cent of its pre-war production capacity by the end of the war, switching to back-up generators in Liverpool, Nottingham and Ipswich where the industrial energy grid had been cut off and converting to oil-fired boilers to get around the shortage of coal. Post-war plans were for more factories, more cigarettes, more tobacco trade with America and the Empire.

Lord Dulverton, Imperial's chairman, said in his 1947 AGM review that 'future prospects' were 'always the most difficult part of a company chairman's speech'. He chose to focus on the immediate worry of sourcing enough tobacco, and of managing tough taxes.

'Tobacco is a comfort and solace and it has a beneficial effect on morale,' he said, hoping that the government might relent on some of its levies. That Golden Virginia, fifteen years later, would share a stable with Golden Wonder shows how wise he was not to plot too far into the future. Crisps, as it turned out, were a far more sustainable solace than cigarettes.

4

cheese and onion

The word CRISPS blows eastward in superheroic red and gold lettering across Manhattan's cheese and onion packets, a typographical affirmation that this word can and should evoke a semi-serious mood of marvel. Lo and behold the *CRISPS*.

Underneath the word a photograph of five crisps floats mid-packet against thick black plastic, poised elegantly for some decorous destiny, interlocked like the Olympic Rings. The crisps inside are what you'd maybe call toothsome: unfashionably thick-cut for non-kettle cooked, not as winsomely pale as most crisps are these days, and not as crunchy to the bite, either. They taste like pub crisps, and I have no complaints. Coupled with a pint of Guinness, they would be a good-value refreshment, if not total nutrition.

I had bought the Irish Manhattans on my way to the Eatyard Crisp Festival in Dublin, nearing lunchtime on a Saturday in August that was sunny and then rainy and then, in cloudless flashes, absolutely roasting.

For a minute of shelter, I put my head inside Ormsby's newsagents on the North Circular Road. And there, almost greeting customers at the door, were the crisps. Where a British newsagent might have chocolate and mints and sweets ranged in the weak-resolve shelves underneath the till, here this prime space was reserved for an apron of Irish crisps. And not a range of crisps, but a range of cheese and onion crisps.

Getting closer, I could see Manhattan, King and Tayto branding, in different shapes and ridges, but all in the same partnership – cheese and onion. I bought one of each cheese and onion kind, and then went into more food shops around the neighbourhood of Phibsborough, putting on and taking off coat layers, trying to see if cheese and onion was a flavour bias pursued only by Ormsby's. Based on this small sample, it wasn't.

I've been to Dublin many times to see old friends who live there but never stopped before to scrutinise the crisp retail arrangements. Cheese and onion, the Eatyard festival organisers later told me, is 'the elite, the classic' in a country that has great dairy produce, a history with potatoes and a sincere love of crisps. 'It's a unison of a thing,' Alanna Burke from the Eatyard team said, of the pervasive Irish fondness for potato crisps. (I couldn't help but notice that when the popular Irish actor Paul Mescal discussed his fashion sense with *Esquire* magazine, he pointed out that he had once worn Gaelic football shorts with a shell top, Ray-Bans, Stan Smith trainers and a packet of prawn cocktail in one hand: 'the full look', in his words. The implication – to my ears anyway – was that the crisps completed his outfit.)

Ireland also lays claim to a tangible boast: it is the birthplace of cheese and onion crisps, the national home of a taste that would be copied and fought over in the crisp industry for decades to come. Its importance can't be overstated: even today, it is the top-selling flavour of Walkers Crisps.

In March 1954, the year meat rationing ended, Tayto debuted a tin of cheese and onion crisps on the Dublin market, a flavour hit that quickly generated headlines and copycats. ('Often imiTAY-TOed, never equalled', ran a 1962 ad in the *Irish Times*.)

Walkers Crisps followed later in 1954 with its own take on a combination until then better known as a filling for sandwiches, pies and pasties. In English crisp lore, the rustic inspiration of a 'ploughman's lunch', a hearty and humble cheese and onion sandwich, seems to have been added later as a patriotic but errant piece of marketing.

All this happened in the first year of business for Tayto, a tiny enterprise brought to life with just £500 by Joseph 'Spud' Murphy. Murphy was a thirty-year-old Dubliner who had turned down a life in the priesthood and dabbled instead in imports of Ribena blackcurrant cordial and the sale of ballpoint pens. Noting that the English-imported crisps he ate were often stale, Murphy went on a field trip to England and came back with the bare minimum of crisp-making knowhow.

In two rented rooms on O'Rahilly Parade back in Dublin, he began to make and pack up salted crisps, which were distributed in tins of eighteen packets around city shops by van. One of his staff, a man from Cloonacool in Sligo named Seamus Burke, recalled being shown around the factory, unimpressed: 'It was a dump but some of Mr Murphy's enthusiasm must have rubbed off on me for when he asked me when I could start, I answered "now".'

Burke joined the company under the illusion that crisps were 'money for jam', as he put it, a way to make profits appear absurdly from thin air. He realised, quickly, that this was wrong. The equipment didn't help: the potatoes were sliced one at a time, and the washed slices were dried in a spin dryer designed for domestic laundry. When loaded with spuds, Burke recalled, it often 'took off from its moorings and flew around the room! Luckily, no one was ever hurt by it.'

A fish-shop fryer did the job of turning slices into crisps. The packets were sealed by gum, hand-painted on by brush. 'Hard slogging,' Burke admitted. Shopkeepers were unconvinced, too. A previous entrant to the crisp market had gone bust, and Dublin shops had stocks of stale crisps loitering unsold. 'These crisps were a complete loss to them and they were naturally wary of our product,' Burke wrote.

The break came when Murphy asked Burke to work with him on a new flavour: cheese and onion. Though cheese and onion had been paired up before in the parallel world of pies and sandwiches, to grind them into one powdered flavour but display them as an ampersand partnership on crisp packets was the beginning of a new era. It brought the world of matches and marriages and duets and cognitive dissonance into the realm of crisps, where previously salt had held sole sway. Did cheese and onion work together? Yes. The universal tension that comes from putting two quantities at work together and testing their joint strengths and weaknesses plays into a human curiosity about the consequences of fusion in all senses.

And cheese and onion simply tastes good. Within a decade, this would make Murphy a millionaire, a man who would favour cashmere jumpers and drive around Dublin in a Rolls-Royce, praise in his ear from the Taoiseach.

The success of the powdered cheese and onion flavour worked on by Burke sparked a sales spike for Tayto. Once the logistics of packing and freshness had been overcome with an automatic packing line in the early 1960s, they ran with it.

In 1964, a decade after the first crisps came out of the Tayto fish-shop fryer, Beatrice Foods in Chicago bought a majority stake in the business. In 1972, the brand bought out King Crisps. An old Smith's Crisps plant in Terenure was acquired for what was now a fast-paced profit-maker. Cheese and onion was on to a winner. By 1988, Tayto Group in Northern Ireland had even introduced a successful mail-order crisp service to deliver abroad. Raymond Hutchinson, Tayto's joint managing director, told the *Financial Times*: 'Our cheese-and-onion flavour is world famous. We operate an overseas postal service and you will often find people at airports carrying boxes of our crisps under their arms.'

Regardless of the sales territory or the flag-waving by the brands, flavouring makes crisps an irrevocably international product. A pointed example of this fact comes from the crisp industry in Afghanistan, where the popular brand Mana (think lemon, pepper and vinegar flavours) had to lay off hundreds of staff following the return of Taliban control and subsequent international freezing of financial transfers. It had become too challenging for Mana to get the flavouring from the Netherlands and the potatoes and packaging from Iran, while the Taliban also banned Mana's television advertising, which featured women eating crisps to the sound of music.

Not all flavouring is created equal and almost no flavouring is manufactured at scale underneath a crisp factory roof. At bigger crisp makers, cheffy development teams and trend forecasters come up with ideas in-house, and they are worked up in experimental kitchens, also in-house. But the seasonings themselves are produced elsewhere, and the ability to do so lies in advanced food science that is beyond the scope of crispers.

Oil, too, is usually imported, although some farm-based crispers may produce enough of a relevant crop to make their own, such as Just Crisps in the UK, which uses its own rapeseed oil. Even the crispers who choose to use cheeses and onions with a specific local provenance require the services of a flavouring house to dry them into a sprayable powder.

Most flavoured crisps are imitations calibrated to resemble natural aromas, whose accuracy and palatability are created by skilled food scientists working at large flavour houses. This expertise is itself competitive, and not strongly represented in Britain, where the uptake of food science courses has steadily been dwindling. The big players are mostly in Europe and America, in particular Switzerland and northern Europe. What's more, the intellectual property of the flavour is difficult to control, sometimes granted under exclusive or time-limited licence to the crispers, but without any concrete way to prevent a competitor from going to a rival flavour house and asking for the same flavour to be made via a different route.

For the existence of food flavourings that parrot complex tastes – from spicy crayfish-flavoured crisps in China and doner kebab crisps in Kazakhstan to salted egg crisps in Thailand – we have in part to thank two British scientists.

In 1941, the British biochemists Archer Martin and Richard Synge, at the Wool Industries Research Laboratories in Leeds, pioneered a new technique for chemical analysis called partition chromatography. This process, at first applied to the amino acids in wool, revealed the make-up of different chemical compounds with unprecedented precision. Martin's collaboration with Synge worked towards advancing pre-existing and more rudimentary techniques for chromatography that had been developed in Russia and Germany. Martin and Synge's goal was to separate and isolate the components of a substance, but to do so with greater accuracy than previously was possible. After experimenting, they achieved a 'partition' of molecules between water, chloroform and silicon.

During the Second World War, this discovery understandably didn't ignite widespread attention. But in 1952 the two men journeyed to Oslo and collected a joint Nobel Prize in Chemistry, in belated recognition of their work. The applications were huge and varied, and for food the possibilities went in two directions – both for verification of possible food adulteration, and for creation of flavouring compounds aided by readings of the chromatographic analysis.

Martin and Synge surely had no intention of revolutionising the world of crisps. But they nonetheless helped to unlock a new horizon of flavour mapping and recreation through skilful combinations of compounds and natural aromas. The potential for novelty was understood by crispers everywhere – barbecue flavour in the United States, for example, followed Tayto's cheese and onion in 1958. The seasoning was launched by a Pennsylvania potato-chip maker called Herr's, which had started in an old tobacco shed on a farm. By the late 1990s, it was turning over $100 million.

As Synge put it in his Nobel lecture: 'The dietitian and food technologist, as well as the pure biochemist, also gain by being able more cheaply and quickly to assay chemically a wide variety of foodstuffs for their essential constituents and to be able to ascertain the effects on these of processing, cooking and so forth.'

The European Union's fruit juice directive of 2012 shows how far this processing possibility could be extended, in theory, by delimiting how far from the original flavour food manufacturers can make a product taste. It stipulates the use of 'suitable processes, which maintain the essential physical, chemical, organoleptic and nutritional characteristics of an average type of juice of the fruit from which it comes'. Apple juice must taste like apples, and must have the mouthfeel of unadulterated apple juice, in other words. There is no such obligation for crisp flavours.

In the 1960s and 1970s, crisp companies plied all their research and development spending power to come up with even more flavours, producing the classics of salt and vinegar, prawn cocktail and roast chicken, among others.

The freedom to conjure such creations from organic compounds meant crisps could now more precisely bear the hallmarks of a place's notions of itself, not just in supposedly nostalgic twinnings such as cheese and onion, but also in the sense of humour that Britain upholds as a badge of national character: a personality gene that would clock 'pigs in blankets' or even Boxing Day curry crisps (from Taylors Snacks, formerly Mackie's) on a Christmas shelf, and at the very least potentially find it mildly amusing.

Emma Wood considers all these questions on a daily basis. Over almost twenty years working for PepsiCo, she has risen to a position of considerable crisp power in the UK: she is the person in charge of new Walkers flavours. 'If you'd told me as a child that my job would involve eating and developing crisps I'd say it was the best job in the world,' she told me. She does not like cheese and onion crisps, but has 'grown to tolerate them'.

The first thing to note about Emma's job is that to create 'flavour' is a broad commercial undertaking, rather than a pick-and-mix selection of ingredients. Conceptually, flavour for crisp insiders is something that happens before, during and after the actual eating, and it is also a sponge for the zeitgeist.

'There's the upfront flavour when you smell or bite, what are you getting, then there's the longevity of the flavour – you don't want it all straight away. And what aftertaste is left in people's mouths?' Emma said. It is the organoleptic consumption of food – the whole-body-in-mind affair. Not just 'What does this taste like?' but also 'How does it make me feel, and how long will I remember it for?' For businesses, there's a final question of importance related to flavour: will I want it again?

For the past eight years Emma has been leading the flavour and seasoning department at Walkers' factory complex in Leicester, a team that consists of about fifteen people and covers the key crisp audiences of UK and Europe. There's also a team in Turkey ('a different market in regulation and taste profiles', she explained) and two more in Asia and Africa, which come under the Lay's branding. The global research and development centres are based in Leicester because 'our biggest [crisp] factory is over the road', but the teams swap and combine knowledge.

Naturally, they talk in crisp lingo. 'The seasoning dusts the crisp – we call it a curtain,' she noted. While the crisps are being tumbled around in a drum, seasoning falls off vibrating plates. How long the crisps are in the drum and the angle of the drum are both important considerations for the end coating. 'It needs to be a nice fine curtain, to mix it gently, but if it's too fine the factory will hate us because it creates dust. We want a sweet spot of a nice uniform curtain and a gentle tumbling motion,' Emma said.

Shape is another component of flavour. The 'great Walkers flat base', as they refer to it, is sort of like a classic shoe last, used for the leading dozen flavours. 'If we're creating a new flavour, and the base is already there, then great,' Emma says, 'but where we really need strong partnership with the factory is if we need a different cut. If we're looking at a different slice, we need to work out what kind of flavour works.'

Everything goes in a straight line in production until the fried potatoes reach the flavour stage, which makes it easier to slip in new ideas at the end of the run, without excessive fiddling with the rest of the settings. PepsiCo juggles hundreds of local *terroir* crisp flavours globally (Lay's mustard mayonnaise in the Netherlands, for one), but for Walkers there are just a core dozen to worry about. Limited-time offerings come on top, while new 'bases' are added in the form of ridges, crinkles, twists and non-potato ingredients. Novelties such as baked bean flavour for Comic Relief, or coronation chicken, which Walkers put together for the king's coronation in 2023, can be turned around in as little as six weeks.

But to create a new commercial launch flavour is still no small matter. It would take, ideally, around three to six months at the least, and that is not including the time absorbed by continuous crystal-ball gazing pursued by in-house teams of flavour analysts. The information they examine spins off consumer and culinary trends, extruded into marketing insights, and it looks at least five or ten years into the future. This doesn't mean that what will be fashionable as a flavour will work on a crisp, Emma noted. 'We're really looking for what will land well. Yes, trend info is interesting but we need to make sure it will work. For example, kimchi is a trendy flavour but in certain places it will be niche; we're looking for loved flavours but not pushing it too far.'

To judge what this might taste like, there is a test kitchen within the factory where skilled chefs cook dishes inspired by restaurants and map out which flavours work best with potatoes. They recently tried multiple attempts at a hot dog and ketchup flavour, but it was ultimately deemed 'too fancy', and didn't go anywhere.

For Walkers some seasonings are made in the UK and some in mainland Europe, through a global partnership with the big flavour houses. They 'bring the flavour to life as a seasoning', Emma said, and Walkers then uses an expert panel in-house, who judge the prototype. 'Once we've validated that, we will send product into people's houses across the country in a balance of genders and ages.' This will inevitably generate variable feedback, depending on the territory of the testers. 'There's lots of differentiation in liking – Scotland has a huge preference for vinegary and pickled flavours, for example.'

On the question of salt, Emma agrees it is 'complicated; it's performing so many roles. We are looking at other foods and ingredients that will drive succulence around bringing that salivation, what helps your brain go, "This is tasty."'

The Bernard Shaw is not a pub. It's more of a barn with a pub inside it, and at the weekend it has a busy, face-flushing, fun-max atmosphere. (That's the best I can do to describe the feeling of being surrounded by 'the craic'.)

It sits just dipped below Cross Guns Bridge in Drumcondra, over the narrow Royal Canal that used to run passengers and freight to and from Dublin's central Docklands out and back to Longford in the west.

Inside there's a confusion of staircases and mezzanines and outdoor lower and upper spaces that seem to sink and raise your footsteps like a ready-made pubsickness. Hard to know where the ground is any more, even with the ceiling in the main room open double-height to the rafters. If you tip your head backwards you can see the lettering of O'Donnells crisp boxes stored up in the eaves, stacked higher and higher and higher until the last box touches the beams. It's like a choir at a church, with the supplies from the Golden Vale in Tipperary looking celestially down on the crowd.

Through a hatch on one side you can order Smithwick's Irish ale or Five Lamps lager or cider or espresso martinis, among other things. These were pouring out from the shakers and taps every minute during the third Eatyard Crisp Festival, when I got there at lunchtime on that August Saturday.

Below the disco ball in the mezzanine, where crisp proceedings were to take place, a basset hound named Earl sat with his owner in the front row, and a hundred or so crisp fans sat behind them. On a dais fringed by huge banana plants, a small table set with a short tablecloth and three bentwood chairs awaited some form of crisp ritual, with a wooden wine case from Portugal filled expectantly with dozens of shiny packets.

When the female emcee announced the start of the onion ring challenge, a bit of clapping and chanting came forward, and Earl looked up from the floor. Three female contestants volunteered, and took their seats, while the emcee set a timer for sixty seconds as the trio started ripping open the packets and stuffing onion crisp rings down on their fingers, like promises of marriage to an invisible crisp betrother, five or six engagements per digit. All this looked familiar; the principle is exactly the same as wearing as many Hula Hoop rings on both hands as possible, a challenge I had confronted many times as a child.

The winner, Carla, held up her hands with nineteen fluffy orange snack tyres wedged on to them, and the emcee applauded 'a fantastic display of crisp-chip fandom'. This, Alanna Burke had told me just before, was 'to ease them into it', the real highlight of the day being the crisp sambo competition, to follow shortly, like the high jump. ('Sambo' is the Irish shorthand for sandwich. In Scotland, it's known as a 'piece and crisps'.)

'Are you a smasher or a squasher?' is the question Alanna said was the top of crisp sambo-eating dilemmas, on whether or not to leave the crisps intact in curls or press them down before eating. The latter for me, but both are satisfying.

The crisp sandwich, it would appear, is a peculiarly British and Irish tradition. Nowhere else seems to have the smash or squash question culturally understood across a population. Walkers Crisps even confirmed to me in an interview that they keep crisp sandwiches in mind when making their classic flavours. 'It can't be too overpowering,' was their phrase.

Pennsylvanian crisp maker Herr's is the only international brand I could find that seems committed to crisp sandwiches, to the extent that it even has a line of 'Sandwi-chips' in flavours such as mustard, ketchup and sweet onion. Their flavour approach goes in the opposite direction to Walkers, dialling up the strength for sandwiches, rather than notching it down. There's even a recipe ideas section on their website for a range of Sandwi-chips, specifying whether the crisps should be squashed or not.

In 2015, the world's first (and to my knowledge, only) crisp-sandwich cafe opened in Belfast, a brief but much talked-about pop-up run by Andrew McMenamin after a joke idea took hold as something more serious. Simply Crispy's sandwich assembly line was stocked with dark-crusted Belfast baps and an array of Tayto Group crisps, plus Monster Munch and other nostalgic classics. 'Ham and cheese and onion Tayto in a Belfast bap was easily the most popular,' McMenamin told the *Irish Mirror* on opening day.

Similarly, by the time the clock hit 4 p.m. at the Bernard Shaw, the moment the crisp sambo bout was supposed to start, a large crowd had gathered underneath the crisp festival bunting. Faces appeared at the balcony, and it was suddenly standing room only at the back. A heavy shower broke the muggy atmosphere outside, sending a theatrical blast of wind and rain clattering through the patio doors.

The emcee approached the microphone. She acknowledged how much everyone was looking forward to this event. 'But', she went on, 'I don't have any bread. Once we have the supplies, it will happen.' A silence rode around the room briefly before it was accepted that this oversight was a liveable one, and not a cause for mutiny.

Some twenty long minutes later, a man came running in with a loaf of Brennans white sliced bread freshly bought from Tesco, out of breath like a dashing post rider delivering a stay of execution. New volunteers were readied again, to be judged by a child volunteer named Jasmine.

Perhaps because of the wait, or the drink, or the heat, or because of all of it, the sambo-making on stage almost instantaneously became a torrid chaos. The contestants ripped at bread and daubed smears of mustard, shovelling crisps at their creations and flinging in second-thought wafers of pink cured meats. By the time sixty seconds had elapsed, the world seemed to have changed its footing, replaced by a new order of crumpled bread jammed with ham, crisps and butter. Exposed copper ducts snaking around the ceiling seemed as if they might blow out the room's hot air at any minute.

Jasmine the judge worked her way along the sambos, critiquing the butter-to-crisp-to-cheese ratios. She proclaimed the youngest competitor, a four-year-old named Roise on the knee of her mother, the winner for a daring combo of cheese and onion Tayto, Edam cheese, pickles, and smoky bacon Tayto on the side.

At Dublin airport on the way home, I sat in the lounge for my delayed flight, trying to measure out the wait slowly through a large bag of Keogh's cheese and onion. I felt a little off. Not because of the Keogh's – they are a nice flaky crisp trimmed with potato skin and a good coating of powdered flavour. And not because I had, all told, eaten about seven packets of crisps in half a day, although that probably didn't help.

Some strangeness had come from an afternoon in a roomful of crisp fans, where it was impossible not to notice that every reference flew a distance over my head. I knew very few of the insider jokes. Even less about the jibes over King versus Tayto crisps (supposedly one of them is inferior). I knew nothing about the nostalgia the Irish crisps brought into the competition. I began to do exactly what ticket-holders for the festival were told not to do: I was taking crisps seriously.

But at the least it stayed with me, this idea, and by the time the plane landed in Glasgow it had become a question. Without the cultural footnotes, was I exactly tasting cheese and onion the same way that everyone else was at the Bernard Shaw? Could I eat twenty, a hundred, three hundred more packets of Irish cheese and onion crisps, and not know what they tasted like?

If this is the case, then a lot gets lost in crisp translation. What's so good about these, an American might equally ask, when eating a bag of British crisps. And vice versa, when we hit the flimsy soft crackle of American Lay's. But they're not tasting the bits that aren't inside the packet, and neither are we.

In the UK, the colour coding of crisps, which is strictly speaking part of their ephemera, became tangled up in the actual taste. Cheese and onion are sold by Walkers in blue packets – a point of contention and confusion among some customers, since most other brands sell salt and vinegar crisps in a blue livery, and cheese and onion in green. The polling body YouGov even put this question to the public, and found that most people believe Walkers must have swapped the packaging colours of its salt and vinegar and cheese and onion flavours at some point.

The problem is significant enough to warrant a statement on the Walkers website FAQ: 'Our Salt & Vinegar and Cheese & Onion flavour crisps packs have always been the colours they are today. Contrary to popular belief, we've never swapped the colours around, not even temporarily. We've no plans to change these designs, as they're signature to our brand.'

Blind tests have shown that our unconscious certainty about blue packaging equalling salt-and-vinegar-flavoured crisps can be so deep it overrides what we'd otherwise know simply through our taste buds. Charles Spence, an experimental psychologist at the University of Oxford, reported that his research with Betina Piqueras-Fiszman showed 'consumers responded more slowly, and made more errors, when they had to pair the color and flavor that they implicitly thought of as being "incongruent" with the same response key'. In other words, the packaging known to loyal brand consumers becomes so hardwired it alters their taste perceptions. 'In addition, when participants tried the two types of crisps from "congruently" and "incongruently" colored packets, some were unable to guess the flavor correctly in the latter case.'

Long after Walkers' then owner Nabisco took over Smith's then owner Associated Biscuits in 1982, the popular Smith's snack Squares was put through a consumer testing process by PepsiCo (the new owner) to gauge reactions to a possible rebranding. Larry Bush, technical brand manager for Squares at the time, told me: 'We knew the cities that loved Squares the most were Leeds and Glasgow. So I trotted off to focus groups with two-way mirrors in both cities.'

They asked the panellists three main questions, the first being whether anyone minded the name changing from Smith's to Walkers.

Another concept was, 'What if we changed the colours of the Smith's blue salt and vinegar to Walkers green salt and vinegar?', and finally, 'What if we do a tartan pattern on it?' The answers were clear: Smith's to Walkers – 'no problem at all'. The tartan idea was tolerable, too. But changing from blue to green: 'Absolutely no way, we'll never buy it again.' It was the nearest thing you could get to a riot in a focus group. There was such a strength of feeling.

Crisps were more than they seemed, wherever they were consumed.

5

into a machine

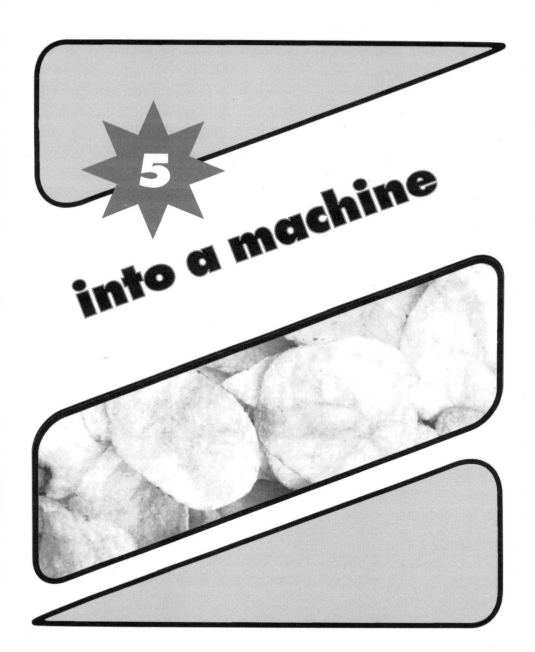

The last time Una Chandler ate a packet of crisps was more than half a century ago. She lost the appetite for them after three years spent working in Winnersh, Berkshire, inside the factory for Crimpy Crisps, a now departed brand that was thriving in the early 1960s when she joined. 'I don't eat crisps because I've seen how they are made,' she told me. 'I don't buy them.'

Long since demolished and replaced by a gigantic Sainsbury's supermarket, the Winnersh factory built by Crimpy's original Scottish owners lives on as a fondly remembered ghost in local online message boards. In the quiet Berkshire village at the crossroads to Reading, the tall white oblong factory was a landmark, tinged with enough elegance to pass for a piece of art deco architecture.

When she answered my phone call, Una had just mowed her lawn in a sunny break of wet summer weather. To make the most of it, she added, she had popped next door and mowed her neighbour's lawn, too. Una is in her eighties, a working chaplain at Reading Borough Council, and resident in a Berkshire parish near the old Crimpy site. Her telephone line was engaged when I first tried her. After lawnmowing she had remembered she hadn't heard from one of her friends in a while, and called to check up on her. 'Each person has a story to tell,' she said, by way of explanation.

Una was born in Barbados, and emigrated to England in 1961 aged seventeen, hoping to find work. She ate her first apple on the flight to Heathrow, and knew no one when she landed. Her school education in Barbados, she said, would not have been enough to secure her a stable job at home. A generation of Caribbean people was in a similar predicament, the Windrush immigrants so named for the 1948 sailing of HMT *Empire Windrush* from Jamaica to Tilbury docks. The ship, famously, was carrying about a thousand West Indians and a handful of Europeans who came to the UK answering the British government's call for workers eligible for citizenship through the yoke of the new Nationality Act, passed in 1948. (Barbados would not gain independence until 1966.) 'A job was very important, that was the reason why we came to England,' Una said. 'A lot of us couldn't get work at home.'

On arrival she signed on at the labour exchange in Reading, where staff would 'send us somewhere where a job was available', in this case usually in nearby food and food-packaging factories. Huntley & Palmers, the long-established Berkshire biscuit maker, had factories for both its biscuits and its fancy biscuit tins, and there was also a local jam factory where a lot of the workforce had come from the Caribbean. The same was true at Crimpy Crisps, which was acquired by the newly merged Frito-Lay company in 1962, as a toe-dabble into British crisp waters.

'Many of us were sent there. I was coming from Barbados, but other people came from St Vincent, Jamaica, Grenada. There was always work at the crisp factory.'

Una was happy she had found something. 'You were just grateful to get a job in those days.' And her family in Barbados was pleased, too. But, she added, 'They didn't have a clue what I was doing.' To be a pair of factory hands didn't lend itself to letters home. Picking out the browned or spoiled crisps. Bagging the good ones neatly into bags. And then packing up the boxes. The factory was producing some crisps under private label, Una said, and only in two flavours – salted (with salt in sachets) and cheese and onion. The business appeared to be doing 'a booming trade', and the machines were always running. Lorries came and went several times a day. Management, she said, treated the workers well, 'very nice and friendly people', and she was supervised benignly by a 'lady boss', a Mrs Hunt.

The production line was simple. Bags of potatoes were cut open, and the spuds were thoroughly washed and sent up on a roller belt, 'into a machine and a machine' – slicing and then frying and then drying and bagging. Continuous fryers, of which the best examples were manufactured in America, had changed the rhythms of most crisp factories by this point, allowing for significant leaps in production volumes. Una remembers watching the crisps in the fryer, and feeling put off by the volume of bubbling hot oil.

Though it wasn't what you'd call a 'posh place', Una said, it was tidy and safe. Workers had lunch breaks and a place to hang coats and jackets away from the hot oil fumes, and clear instructions about daily tasks. There was no sense, she said, of being treated differently because of where she came from, although this was an acute hazard of emigration for many of the Windrush generation in the UK, particularly the young men who were turned away from job opportunities in the more unsettled economic climate of the 1970s.

The risk for Una was boredom, or getting stuck, making crisps daily, monthly, yearly, without the prospect of advancement.

Many people left quickly, or went back to the labour exchange to look for better-paid work elsewhere. 'People started to move on; they didn't want to continue in that kind of job. Some people then got married or had babies. It was just a way of life. Crimpy Crisps was an open door for Caribbean people. When we came and you didn't have friends, we made friends working in those places.'

Salary was calculated according to age, and since she was a teenager, Una took home just over £5 (about £90 today) a week. 'That was our whole ambition – to earn money. If you could find a job with even £6 you'd move on.' Una's lodgings in Reading were £2.50 a month, and £1.50 was enough to 'fill a trolley full of food' at the supermarket, she recalled. 'Food was cheap. Things were different.'

When she left for work in the mornings, bread loaves were waiting on windowsills, milk bottles on the doorsteps, as if food deliveries belonged to a system of civilised, orderly plenty. Housewives at home were the new target market for crisp advertising, in charge of household budgets, while the workforce at the crisp factory was largely made up of young immigrant women.

Crimpy Crisps would send a coach to pick up some workers from St Mary's Shopping Centre in Reading, stopping along the route to pick up others. Una set off to meet the coach around 6.30 or 7 a.m., to arrive at the factory by 8 a.m. It was a sociable commute – the workers all talked to each other – and her young age made her the 'little sister' of the group. 'The West Indians were there to work, we all had the same mindset. It didn't matter if one person was from Barbados or from Jamaica. We became friends.'

Una had her first of six children in 1963, and decided she would never eat crisps again, a vow she has stuck to. 'Those crisps are cooked in a lot of oil,' she said, almost with an audible shaking of her head down the phone line.

As we spoke, Una said memories were filtering back to her, some that made her laugh with surprise. She had not talked about the 'crisp years' for quite some time. Factory work, she observed, is often looked down on, and not discussed openly, but she felt strongly that there was 'nothing to be ashamed about'.

'In those days you didn't find many English women going out to work. They were at home as nannies; maybe teenagers worked, but you wouldn't find many adult women getting up in the morning to go out to work, they were mostly housewives.'

This contrasted to the Caribbean community, she said, where one woman would become the childminder for other women, and most mothers went back to work. It cost under £2 a week to pay the childminder five days a week, Una noted. For all of the women at Crimpy Crisps, the factory was a first chapter. 'It was the beginning of our future. Then we made our way.'

Looking at the forty-year trend for the female workforce in the UK, the Institute for Fiscal Studies reported that women born in 1958 were 'only half as likely to be in work one year after the birth of their first child as one year before'. For women born in 1970 'only around one-third moved out of paid work when the first child arrived'. The rise in educational attainment for women ran in parallel with their rising engagement in full-time work.

Manufacturing, however, has declined in the UK steadily over the past forty years, and flatlined in the past decade. In 1978, there were 6.7 million manufacturing jobs in the UK, but only 2.6 million in 2023. On the crisp-factory floor, this means the ever-thinning presence of humans. Automated technology with light supervision from human eyeballs has become the norm.

PepsiCo's new multi-million-dollar crisp factory in Assam, India, is a rare example of engineered recruitment with an explicit gender focus in the workforce. When it opens in 2025, three-quarters of the workers will be women, PepsiCo says, a pledge that it has made in partnership with the local government to improve women's economic empowerment. PepsiCo India president Ahmed ElSheikh said they 'anticipate a transformative impact on Assam's entire ecosystem', in which many jobs currently rely on the tea industry.

PepsiCo has scaled quickly in India and Asia. The company said, in language reminiscent of Big Crisp speak, that it was 'expanding penetration across the nation'. But this has not been without controversy. In 2021, a dispute broke out over who owned the rights to produce a particular potato, the FL 2027 variety used for Lay's crisps. PepsiCo wanted to register its trademark for this prized potato in the growing Indian market, but Indian law does not automatically recognise intellectual property as applied to genetic agronomic material. In other words, if Indian farmers had FL 2027 tubers, they were free to grow them for whichever company or purpose they pleased. This held until PepsiCo appealed again, successfully, in early 2024, when the Delhi High Court decreed that a previous ruling revoking PepsiCo's patent registration for FL 2027 no longer stood.

The debate has not changed the fact that there is still a need for workers who will, among other chores, change and clean the slicing blades, move and empty the bins, occasionally stir the 'hand-cooked' crisps, cellophane-wrap boxes on pallets and pick and taste random samples off the line – jobs that, for the time being at least, would be costly and clumsy to replace with automation. Stiff-armed robots cannot eat, taste or describe crisps, at least not yet.

The Winnersh factory was knocked down. Crimpy Crisps had not been the route to the British market that Frito-Lay had hoped for. Plenty more crisp factories were closed in this period. In the exploratory and expanding trade of the postwar period, crisps seemed to achieve two kinds of impossible. First, from standing starts, new entrants could be selling tens of thousands of boxes within years of trade. And just as quickly, they would fold or sell out, dissolving hundreds of jobs at a time, as if the appetite for daily tonnes of crisps could blow away like wrappers in the wind. One man, John Mudd, saw all of this happen first hand.

On Saturday afternoons as a boy in 1950s Cardiff, John used to take himself to the local cinema for the 'Tanner Rush' matinee, so named for the sixpence admission fee. This showtime always drew long queues for tickets, he said, a clamouring for laughs from Laurel and Hardy and the Three Stooges, or for the excitement of cowboys and Indians cantering up dust through the Wild West.

Instead of popcorn, the cinema tuck shop sold packets of salted Smith's crisps to schoolboys like John. Children would often cry out during the film that they had gone stale, John remembered, and worse yet, that the salt sachets had become damp (backing up what the Walkers marketing director said in the *FT*). The crisps were delivered to the cinema in tins, about twenty-four packets inside each one, and if the packets were left outside in the cold hall of the cinema overnight it was seemingly enough to take the crunch off the crisp. Smith's didn't suffer any fallout, to judge by their dominance in British life – they were visible everywhere from the cinema to the roads. 'Smith's had a rack on top of their vans for the tins and they used to have a sign on the back that read, "Toot your horn if you like Smith's crisps,"' John said.

He thought little more about crisps until the early 1970s, when he filled in some shifts at Smith's for a friend who had gone on holiday. The gig was van selling boxes of crisps around shops and grocers in the valleys of South Wales, unpacking orders, taking new ones and making small talk with the grocers. He did it so well that he was offered a permanent position straight away, and began to wear in his sales route, out west to Porthcawl and east towards the Severn Bridge, stopping to take orders at Lipton, Fine Fare and smaller branches of Tesco. 'It was a good gig. We'd sell as much as we could, and it was a weekly wage. And five days a week, no weekends, which was a beauty.'

At this stage, Walkers wasn't quite a national brand. (Even Walkers' former CEO Martin Glenn, in his book *The Best Job in the World*, said that when PepsiCo acquired the Walkers business, 'we

A 1930s advertising booklet for Smith's Crisps. The increasing popularity of picnics worked in crisps' favour.

A typical 1940s crisp packet in waxy paper. Early crisps contained no additives – only oil and salt.

Marilyn Monroe and Tom Ewell with a cameo from a bag of
Bell's Potato Chips in *The Seven Year Itch* (1955).

A family picnic in New England, 1958, with a bag of State Line Potato Chips. The brand's Connecticut birthplace, Enfield, neighboured Massachusetts.

A 1950s advert for Seabrook Crisps, based in Bradford. Different areas of the UK have flavour preferences. Salt and vinegar, for example, is hugely popular in Scotland.

Right: A worker at the Golden Wonder warehouse in Bothwell, 1970. The boxes promise a special offer of 'free tights'; it was then common among crisp brands to flaunt gifts and toys that could be exchanged for packet coupons.

Below: A 1970s English pub session. Public houses were once crisps' biggest marketplace.

A delivery of Ready Salted crisps to the village shop in St Just, Cornwall, 1970. Delivery drivers often doubled up as salesmen.

Mary Berry on a panel judging specimens of crisp, 1977.

You could eat a million

Tried Salt & Vinegar? Smokey Bacon?
Cheese & Onion? Roast Chicken?
Whatever the flavour,
Golden Wonder are so much crisper
you could eat a million.
And still want more.

GOLDEN WONDER CRISPS

A 1969 advert for Golden Wonder, which started as a sideline
to an Edinburgh bakery in 1947.

A persuasive beer mat. Advertising became the toughest battleground of the so-called 'crisp wars'.

Former England footballer Gary Lineker in a promotion for Walkers Crisps in 1994.

had an undeniably great product, but it wasn't yet a great brand . . .
It was imperative for us to get ourselves some truly memorable
advertising.') Golden Wonder was the main and only nationwide
competitor to Smith's, backed by Imperial Tobacco's deep pockets
for television advertising. John rose up through the Smith's management ranks, becoming a sales rep and then area sales manager,
before ditching crisps briefly in the 1980s to sell fitted kitchens. He
returned to the industry in the early 1990s with a job offer from
Bensons Crisps, a relative newcomer that had got going in 1977.
But when, to John's annoyance, Bensons closed the Newport factory where they produced their hand-cooked crisps line, he decided
to go it alone, starting his own company trading as Real Crisps.

With a patchwork of loans and finance he bought up the equipment from an old Bombay mix factory in the Midlands, which he
got up and running in a new, small production site in Wales. He
started van selling in the valleys again, just as he had twenty years
before, but the hand-cooked product was a 'bit greasy' as a result
of the suboptimal tunings of the elderly Bombay mix cooker. He
had at least a point of difference to Kettle Chips, which marketed
themselves in big bags for 'cocktail parties', whereas Real Crisps
were in small individual packets, aimed at adults in pubs and
independent shops. Yet without a cash injection, the business was
soon 'running on the buffers'.

'The bank said forget it.' John turned instead to a company on
the same industrial estate that catered for hospitality, and they
'chucked in £50,000 and underwrote our expenditure, and took 80
per cent of the shares'. Growth after this boost was dynamic, John

recalled, enabling Real Crisps to buy 'proper cookers from America', and move into bigger premises. The company started to get some private-label business with Somerfield, and then with Asda.

> By this time we were doing OK and then had to move to an even larger place, and took a place near Pen y Fan, 6,500 square feet. We spent a million and a half getting it kitted out with eight cookers from America. These were computer controlled and had a stirring system, though we had a man with a rake who caught the missed crisps. We were churning out three hundred kilos an hour.

Bensons meanwhile closed altogether in 2001, falling into receivership with the loss of more than three hundred jobs. It had discovered the hard edges of the industry, and the problem of keeping up with the likes of Walkers and Golden Wonder. Its factories made their passage to scrapbook photos of online nostalgia.

In 2007, John's co-directors at Real Crisps decided they too wanted to sell the business. It was bought by Tayto Group and John received 16 per cent of the deal: 'Retrospectively, I'm disappointed. At the time, as a council house boy, someone's waving £1.3 million under your nose, I got a bit excited.'

Tayto Group is a large player in the 'private label' business, making crisps for other businesses in bespoke packaging. For a smaller fryer like Real Crisps, private label had proved a strange ability to be both a boost and a vulnerability. When John Mudd secured the deal with Asda, for example, the volume then represented half of Real Crisps' business – a 'big knife edge', as he put it. It was not a buffer but a burden, and subsequent efforts were all focused on reducing the dependency on Asda's contracts.

Because so many of the 'craft' crispers have been bought up by conglomerates, which encourage them to produce private label for supermarkets, there is a blurred line – not visible to the consumer at eye level – between the presence of own-brand and branded crisps. It's testament to the potency of marketing and design that the latter are still perceived as more desirable.

Though the scales of production have grown, this is nothing new. In 1957, Meredith & Drew was producing crisps for Marks & Spencer, alongside its giant range of biscuits. It was one of the biggest manufacturers of crisps in the UK, but barely anyone had heard of it. M&S was posh, but M&D was not. It was invisible.

If you turn to the back of a packet of Marks & Spencer crisps today, you will see most of them are made in the UK. M&S had to apologise in 2023 after it was reported to Trading Standards for a packet that boasted '100 per cent British potatoes' but also printed the caveat that not all the potatoes were guaranteed to be British, a consequence of the 2022 drought, M&S later explained.

The wider complexity is acknowledged even by the biggest player of them all, Walkers.

'None of the equipment manufacturers solely make for us, and there are things out there that are quite closed,' Chris Dimelow of PepsiCo's potato and tortilla platform told me. 'The world of crisps has become complicated. One of the things that we don't know is how anyone is making their product in terms of private label. We don't know who is making what product for who.'

These days, John Mudd will buy the odd packet of crisps at the golf clubhouse. 'They are forty grams and they want £1.25, which is bloody scandalous.' He remembers that when Bensons was a PLC, it often had investors 'poking around'. They used to say 'crisps were sexy because they were inflation proof. Now you will always have someone on offer. Who does the special offer gets the volume.'

Crisp prices rose 13 per cent in the twelve months to July 2023 for individual packets, and by 19 per cent in the same period for multipacks. 'Shrinkflation' – fewer crisps, more air, same packet sizes – is also a reputational problem for crisps. Like John I double-take at a packet of crisps that costs more than £1, so ingrained is the idea of crisps as a small-change treat. Anything above seems like an unwelcome message from the future – as if one day I might be browsing photos of more shuttered factories online, more ghosts in the machine.

6

prawn cocktail

P rawn cocktail, as a prepared dish, was a feature of dinner-party suavity in 1970s British society, which was more adventurous in its food tastes than ever before. Blushing a rose colour from the cocktail-stem glasses in which it was served, prawn cocktail spoke of exotic flair borrowed from the casinos and bars of America, where it was first popularised. Shelled prawns, mayonnaise, tomato and paprika (or a variation of the same) quickly became a people-pleasing, showy starter for guests at home, and was widely touted on restaurant menus, too.

Indeed, prawn cocktail was so fashionable that people were soon questioning whether it was in fact unfashionable. Delia Smith, in her 1978 *Complete Cookery Course*, declares the prawn cocktail already over. In her chapter on 'Pâtés and Starters', she snubs it entirely and lists instead a recipe for avocado and seafood salad, declaring it 'a distinct improvement on the inevitable prawn cocktail as a starter'. (Her 'yoghurt seafood sauce' for this alternative recipe doesn't immediately inspire me, personally.)

Prawn cocktail crisps, meanwhile, as an imitation of something 'posh' or a bit fancy, were an excellent demonstration of crisps' capacity for sly humour. The new flavour of prawn cocktail crisps emerged on the British scene in the early 1970s with KP's Disco shells and Skips, both extruded snacks in novelty shapes. It was a sign of how socially reactive the product had become.

The just-sour, just-creamy and spicy prawn kick worked undeniably well with the starchiness of potatoes. Prawn cocktail crisps were delicious. But the new flavour also undercut the supposed exclusivity of a food taste. Prawn cocktail for all, the crisp flavour seemed to wink mischievously at the dinner-party-going classes. Food prices had risen in 1970s Britain by over 300 per cent in the space of decade. Delia Smith referenced the problem of the 'dizzying climb' of food prices in the preface to her *Cookery Course*, declaring that the 'really affluent era of food is passing'. The post-war recovery and prosperity of the 1950s and 1960s had hit a barrier.

The late Gerald Kaufman, Labour MP for Manchester Ardwick, asked in a 1973 session of Parliament how ordinary people were supposed to deal with swingeing food-price rises. 'Are the government determined to price proteins out of the diet of my constituents? Do they suggest that my constituents should eat ice cream, lollies and potato crisps for their main meals?'

In the light, melt-on-the-tongue formula, Skips and Discos also recalled Chinese prawn crackers, and so reflected another part of changing British society. The arrival of Hong Kong Chinese people from the late 1950s onwards brought Britain an entirely new experience of food. Chinese food entrepreneurs such as Wing Yip, who settled from Hong Kong in 1950s Yorkshire, found that his English customers were as begrudging (and sometimes prejudiced) as they were curious about his cooking.

'Food is a culture – you cannot change people in one year. In those days, in the 1950s, I think a lot of people never had Chinese food before.' He noted how Chinese restaurants were among the few places open after 9.30 p.m. for food, and how there was at first a reciprocal adaptation in the menu, with Chinese chefs serving spiced noodles and curries alongside mixed grills and chips (not rice), to appease a Yorkshire–Hong Kong hybrid palate. People would stare at the menu from the window outside, he said, and they would say, '"sweet and sour pork", everybody think, "sweet and sour pork? Sweet and sour?" They are very sarcastic. They couldn't understand how can a thing be sweet and sour at the same time. Until they taste it.'

British affection for Chinese foods grew slowly, then embedded firmly, and became clumsily appropriated in KP and Golden Wonder's packaging for 'Oriental'-style snacks. Today it is more of a can't-live-without addiction. This is a repeated pattern of food culture in the UK – just as Wing Yip said, 'you cannot change people in one year'. The irony is that the concept of sweet and sour is about the fierce power of opposites, a concept that is everywhere in crisps – and that takes no time, in blood and brains, to be understood.

European Commissioner Martin Bangemann in 1991 unwittingly put his foot into the British prawn cocktail passion and got rebuked accordingly. In a European Commission draft proposal for a directive on the use of sweeteners and additives in food, a clause directed that no sweetener should be added to crisps, which would have wiped out the formula for prawn cocktail powdering at the time. Uproar followed.

The prawn cocktail jeopardy (not to be confused with the 'prawn cocktail offensive' or 'prawn cocktail circuit', as the Tories dubbed Labour's 1990s wooing of the corporate sector) appeared to be the result of an omission by the civil service to include flavoured crisps on an agreed list of British food that should be exempt from the new legislation. MPs rallied to save the prawn cocktail crisp, with an early day motion tabled in Parliament in April 1991:

> That this House deplores the omission of crisps and savoury snacks from the proposed EC sweeteners directive; notes that this omission has no health or scientific justification and that it would risk job losses and jeopardise a United Kingdom market which has developed over the past 15 years and is now worth £70 million a year; and urges Ministers to take all necessary steps to save the great British crisp and ensure that British crisps and snacks of all flavours can continue to be enjoyed by consumers.

It turned out to be hot oil over almost nothing. Bangemann claimed to have never heard of prawn cocktail crisps, and suggested the British would be welcome to hold on to them as a delicacy if this is what they considered to be one. The hard-right Conservative MP Dame Jill Knight, in a 1993 Commons debate, recalled the shenanigans but alluded to the political undertone of the obfuscating media reports around it:

> Some months ago there was a great prawn crisp row because people believed that prawn crisps were to be snatched from their mouths by the vicious interference of Brussels. People wrote to me in great distress because they had been told that Brussels would not allow us to continue to use double-decker buses. That fear was just as fallacious as the one about prawn crisps, but we have gone from crisps to buses to other topics. Such issues,

rather than not being a member of the [European] Community,
are what worry people.

As its name suggested, the European Union promoted unity,
but some bristled at what seemed to be an adjacent theme for
uniformity, enacted through the principles of daily life in every
member state. The press ran with a Euro-myth – one whose
potential was not overlooked by Boris Johnson and the Brexiters
during their 2016 campaigns. We must resist the 'great war against
the British prawn cocktail-flavour crisp', Johnson boomed from
the pages of the *Daily Telegraph*.

Britain is a class society. It can be a snob society. Affluence is not
just a quality of living but a social value in itself. But what about
crisps? Does the rule translate?

It is hard to deny that there are different socially contextu-
alised categories of crisp, at the least. This isn't an exhaustive
list, but to me the main ones are: pub crisps (bog standard, tear
the packet open to share), sandwich crisps (slightly elevated),
party crisps (nothing too fancy), Christmas crisps (ideally the
fancier the better), misery crisps (unwise quantities of whatever
is there), emergency crisps (even larger quantities of whatever is
there) and posh crisps (hand-cooked, interestingly flavoured or
both).

Yet the notion of posh crisps is a triumph of abstract marketing, as much as it is a categorical reality. Today, both the prawn

cocktail dish and the crisp flavour are seen as a classic combination that is well loved, if not wildly popular. Tyrells' Posh Prawn Cocktail crisps, for example, promise 'A retro revival, perfectly piquant with nostalgic flavour and a heartening dash of brandy. So posh you'll need to dust off the finest glassware.'

With grating chumminess, Tyrrells' copywriting voice offers no attempt to disguise the ploy of its 'posh' prawn cocktail flavour. These potato crisps are faux-inviting you into a twee, dated scene of posh living involving brandy and polished glassware. Underneath the joke, however, there seems to be a genuine attempt to distance these crisps from crisps that are below the salt, crisps that don't quite belong in a certain milieu – as if to say, prawn cocktail usually is not posh, but be reassured these crisps are something else. They are posh enough.

Strangely, in Sainsbury's in-house magazine, *JS Journal*, crisps were once written about as if their entire taxonomy lifted them in class terms well above the more proletarian potato. In the February 1964 edition, according to an editorial:

> With the rise of incomes the consumption of cheap, satisfying food has gone down. Potatoes declined steadily until the war years and even in today's affluent society expenditure on them increases as one moves down the social scale; ordinary potatoes that is. New potatoes, which are a delicate and expensive food, come into a different category; so do potato crisps, the sale of which has doubled over the past five years and will continue to rise as additional flavours are brought onto the market. Potato

chips on the other hand, although they can be bought ready prepared, have strong working class associations and are not selling so rapidly.

That crisps were seen as classier than chips is a distinction that was tied to price and to novelty. But also, in a sense, to a madness. Crisps and chips are made from the same thing, but the likelihood in 1964 of sourcing them from very different places on the high street – the supermarket and the chippy – meant that they were worlds apart.

It's relevant to note here that packaging can be the most expensive part of a crisp unit for the manufacturer. The thicker and more protective the film, the higher the cost. Cooking oil, potatoes and seasoning come next, usually in that order of cost. So the 'poshness' is an encasing outer layer, a display of good taste through visual branding and identity. While it is not a physical part of what you eat, it is part of the experience.

The idea of 'posh' crisps is a nuanced form of social imitation that takes poshness itself as something worthy of tongue-in-cheek deference. Poshness is a direct crisp selling point, instead of being poked fun at, as happened with an early noughties Walkers Sensations ad campaign starring Victoria Beckham, Tara Palmer-Tomkinson and others, in a variety of faux-raunchy, faux-snobby skits with the blunt tagline 'Posh crisps from Walkers'. Latterly, poshness has begun to be sold as a treat. Poshness is used brazenly and literally in crisp flavours such as black truffle, whose rich and rare umaminess happens to pair deliciously with potato. Or in champagne- or prosecco-flavoured crisps, which contain no alcohol. Money symbols have found their way into the surface layer of branding.

But can a crisp itself, a fried potato, really be classy? There are a few ways of looking at the question. Take as a guide a Greek philosopher, Socrates, attending a banquet (with grapes, wine and er, no crisps). He reasons with his fellow guests on what the greatest love means, as later recounted by Plato in the *Symposium*. He establishes first that love is 'of' something, which implies its lack. Love of beauty, in his example, means that the thing loving beauty does so because it lacks it.

Applying this to the consumer market, we want the things we don't have – love them, even – and in the case of crisps ascribe to them properties of good taste, social standing and social superiority. From this perspective, posh crisps derive much of their status simply from our belief that such a status exists.

To look at the question in a different way, take a different definition of poshness. Let's assume it's not an absolute value, and has no criteria in place that need to be met. Nothing material qualifies an object as posh or not. Only relativity within the crisp category means that poshness exists, as a comparative quality. It is what the American economist Edward Hastings Chamberlin termed in the 1930s 'product differentiation' in action – competition is enabled and driven by being able to communicate what makes a certain thing different, and perhaps better, than the others on the shelf. Poshness is merely a point on a scale – a distinct identity, but not necessarily a better one. Just different.

The desirability of a product that had limited availability was proved in the other direction by the Whole Shabang, a line of potato chips made by the Keefe Group in the US, which specialises in food and equipment for the 'correctional market', or for inmates in jail. Whole Shabang began as a prison-only brand, not available on the outside. And instead of offering multiple flavours, there is one 'super seasoning' that tastes of many flavours at once. It was enough to make them beloved of those serving time, to the extent that they clamoured for the product to be made publicly available once they had been discharged. (You can now buy them online, at a hefty mark-up.)

Yet another way to look at the question is to judge the answer by asking what poshness is synonymous with, a question that seems to lead inexorably to the middle classes. Poshness is synonymous with the middle class, and/or upper middle class, as they go about their shopping, because it belongs in a lifestyle that is more comfortable than the minimum. Poshness is not a necessity in life. Then this gets into another territory, which is to ask whether the opposite to 'posh' crisps is some form of in-touch-with-reality crisp, a working-classness compared to the non-premium product. I don't know the answer here, but I spoke to someone who once worked at Walkers, who described crisps as divided not by classes but by tribes: this seems close to the truth. That crisp behaviours are tribal, however, doesn't seem to prevent them from also being classist.

The UK launch in 1988 of Kettle Chips, originally hailing from Oregon, was one of the first appearances of a crisp with premium appeal. It had the leverage not of surface-layer branding at first, but something more fundamental to the fried potato itself – the appeal of batch cooking.

Cameron Healy, a food entrepreneur who had sold cheese from a van and traded in margarine, came up with the Kettle Brand potato chip company in 1982 as a 'natural food' that would have clear, clean flavours. Early examples included yoghurt and green onion, or 'no salt', for health.

The 'kettle' method was not a novelty in America at that point, and kettle-cooked chips continue to be made with excellence and abundance in the United States today – indeed, the market of founder-owned premium potato-chip brands in North America is much stronger than it is in the UK. Brands such as Boulder Canyon, Hal's New York, Hen of the Woods and Cape Cod (owned by Kettle Brand owner Campbell's) churn them out in great, imaginative flavours that manage to be not only regional but city-specific too, ranging from dill pickle, sweet onion, buttermilk and chive to sweet mesquite barbecue. When Amazon launched its own snack line, Aplenty, in 2021, it also focused on kettle cooking.

In crispspeak, the word 'kettle' was new enough in the UK in the 1990s to be alluring. The late Canadian food entrepreneur Jon Whiteside, who had grown up on a potato farm, launched his Jonathan Crisp brand in the UK in the late 1990s with the tagline 'Crisps for Snobs', combining the novelty of kettle cooking with the indelibility of British social-status preciousness. The marketing was targeted semi-satirically at an absurdly plummy audience, featuring caricatures of horsy-looking toffs and social-ites in a display of well-dressed, all-white classism that probably would not pass the sniff test today.

This formula, however, of allying visual and/or facial 'char-acters' to crisps has been a repeated technique in British crisp packaging. It can also be seen in John Mudd's hand-cooked brand (now owned by Tayto Group) Real Crisps' faces, which are much more diverse and contemporary, and in Tyrrells' vintage, Land Girl-style iconography of tweeded men and thick-stockinged women, which seems to allude inexplicably to much of postwar social liberation never happening. But just as Tyrrells' descrip-tion of posh prawn cocktail insures itself linguistically against being taken too seriously, so Jonathan Crisp protects itself from an absolute outright declaration of elitism by writing its own self-importance into the tagline 'Crisps for Snobs'. All of this helps to distract consumers from what they are actually buying, which is seasoned fried potatoes.

Consumers accepted that 'kettle' equated to a different class of crisps, and the American language of 'chips' on the packet also endorsed their higher price point at the checkout. Batch-cooked crisps do taste heavier and oilier, unless they are thoroughly spun, and I believe they are more filling than their finely sliced counterparts.

Kettle Chips were sold in big bags with slightly weightier packaging, adorned with a retro serif typeface and a small but dependable range of mildly esoteric flavour combinations. The pairings of premium flavours, such as salt and black pepper, or mature cheddar and red onion, did not deviate far from the classic unions or patriotic overtones that long-standing British crispers adhered to. But they carried emphatic references to a rising new Britishness, and to a more international British palate that was beginning to shrug off an image of stolid, uninspiring, borderline embarrassingly bad cooking.

No other country found itself quite so publicly stuck with a reputation for unappealing and unskilful food preparation. Despite the stigma attached to its waistlines and fast foods, America had its Southern spices, its Latino influences, its high-quality red meat and its fertile produce seeded from coast to coast, while France and the rest of continental Europe had their culinary credentials underwritten by sun-kissed produce and centuries of food skills passed from family to family.

As Britain slowly learned a different mode of food cultivation and food culture, around the turn of the millennium, crisps showed their ability to be expressive of an entire nation's changing tastes. Salt and vinegar, the favourite British combination behind cheese and onion, attained a gastro sea salt and balsamic vinegar or sea salt and malt vinegar makeover.

Similar 'posh' things happened to beef, cheese and onion. Jonathan Crisps' flavours black olive & garlic and horseradish & onion represented two poles of the new British food fashions – the Mediterranean on one side, and the gastropub Sunday roast on the other. Crisps, being an imitative product, can seemingly join and depart from consumer trends with agile ease, not least by adding gourmet vocabulary to flatter (and upsell to) the middle classes.

Tyrrells, as one of the UK's earliest crisp brands to overtly market 'hand-cooked' crisps to the crisp public in 2002, gained an early-mover advantage in this confusing psychological minefield. Established in Herefordshire by the farmer William Chase, it stirred the slices of its own farm's potatoes in small batches of oil, instead of sending them at ruthless throttle down a cooking line.

This was a step change in the premium market, and it produced a stiffer crisp that carried flavour and salt differently, too. The method of crisping, rather than the flavour flair, was now a competitive edge. Hand-cooked crisps, being more expensive to make, also cost more to buy. Crisps were pushing into new market niches.

If ever you have stopped to picture a crisp factory where each potato slice is lovingly hand-cooked, the vision surely has slipped from your mind's grasp quickly, and intuitively. In the Food Safety Act 1990, Section 15 'creates an offence for describing, advertising or presenting food which falsely describes the food or is likely to mislead as to the nature or substance or quality of the food'. This proscription doesn't seem to stretch to use of the term 'hand-cooked', which to me at least evokes a more personalised 'one chef, one crisp' process than is the case on the factory floor. Hands might be here or there, pressing buttons, or occasionally stirring, but kettle/batch cooking is still a partially automated and industrial process. Food companies won't affix the 'hand-cooked' label if there is no human interaction involved whatsoever, but it is still a grey area when you consider the implied method versus the real one.

Tyrrells was also a pioneer of vegetable crisps chipped from carrots, beetroot and parsnips – a healthier alternative to potato crisps, but also cheaper to make. What started as a farmer's 'shed' business enjoyed exponential growth, and then was bought by a series of ever-larger organisations in 2008, 2013, 2016 and 2018, a ricochet of sales that would be echoed in the wider market of independents in the UK. The shed became distant. Tyrrells now carries the line 'Established in Herefordshire' on its packets, without explicitly saying 'Made in Herefordshire'. A longing for rural heritage and 'farm-fresh' quality is left to linger on the packaging.

Pipers Crisps, which started in 2004 with a 'Made by Farmers' tagline, was another fast-growing kettle brand that sat itself in a best-of-British marketing furrow. The trio of Lincolnshire farmers who started Pipers, Alex Albone, Simon Herring and James Sweeting, had vowed not to sell to the big supermarket chains, preferring to keep their brand stocked in smaller shops and delis. A newer hand-cooked crisp brand, Brown Bag Crisps in Surrey, has made the same pledge: to be 'an independent company which supports independent retailers'. In Staffordshire, Just Crisps farms its own rapeseed and Lady Rosetta potatoes to make '100 per cent British' crisps that it also does not offer to supermarkets.

Eventually, the Pipers trio walked away with £20 million when they sold to Walkers in 2018, by which point their company had reached a turnover of £11.4 million. The PepsiCo sale was only possible once the mooted merger had cleared a phase 1 investigation by the Competition and Markets Authority. And categories, if not classes, were key to the overcoming of this hurdle. 'Pipers produces premium potato crisps only, while PepsiCo primarily produces conventional potato crisps,' the CMA investigation found, pressing the green light. Premium and conventional crisps were market realities, but the terms depended on more abstract social classifications of crisps, too, to uphold a difference.

Three years later, Pipers was selling £1 million a month worth of crisps, and its crisps were available in the supermarkets. The tagline changed on most packets to 'Est. by farmers', and there is no longer any mention of hand-cooking anywhere.

And interestingly, though the boundaries are somewhat abstract, the traffic between 'conventional' and 'premium' crisps only seems to go in one direction. The CMA polled PepsiCo and Pipers customers, who 'indicated that conventional crisps are not an alternative to premium potato crisps. Some customers noted that while consumers may switch from conventional to premium potato crisps if the latter's price decreased to the price of the former, there would be limited switching the other way around. For this reason, some customers stated that they would consider buying only premium potato crisps.'

Once a posh crisp person, it seems, always so.

7

we lost things to gain things

One Monday night in September 1988, smoke started billowing from the rooftops of Golden Wonder's factory in Corby, Northamptonshire. When it had been ribbon-cut in the 1960s, the factory was the UK's largest devoted to crisps, and by the time of the great fire it represented almost eight hundred jobs in the local area, sometimes employing several members of the same family at once. A hot-oil feed pipe had apparently malfunctioned, the BBC reported, and the whole building caught alight and blazed down.

This wasn't the last time a crisp factory would become an inferno. In 2012, a worker flicked a lit cigarette in the Real Crisps factory in Crumlin, burning it to a proverbial crisp. Tayto Group made ninety people redundant, left South Wales behind and moved Real Crisps production to its Corby plant. Corkers Crisps in the Cambridgeshire Fens had its production wiped out when a fire swept through all but one of its buildings in May 2020. (It has submitted plans to rebuild.) Walkers itself had a blaze at Leicester in 2021, and so did Tayto Group in 2005 at its Tandragee Castle site. No one was injured in any of these incidents, but the effects on business were profound.

Half of Golden Wonder's national production was gone (along with much of its archival material, sadly). While the company began to rebuild and refinance with a new business plan, Walkers filled out the missing spaces on the supermarket shelves. It cannot have been a welcome way for anyone to get ahead, but Walkers now found itself with an opportunity to seize. Its sales jumped accordingly, and in 1989 PepsiCo-owned Frito-Lay swooped in and bought the business for $1.35 billion. The timing was also strategic, designed to strengthen PepsiCo's position in anticipation of the single market in the newly constituted European Union. According to a contemporary report in the *New York Times*: 'PepsiCo said Walkers and Smith's would help it establish a solid European base in 1992, when trade barriers between European Community countries will be dissolved.' In this broader political light, the story of crisps as a primarily British business boast seems to take another helix turn: like the curl of a Quaver, it was never a straight line. PepsiCo wanted to create a European crisp fortress, and to do so it built out Walkers as a British national brand first, through its acumen and deep pockets for marketing.

The 1980s had been the last era of Walkers as a 'small' business, or at least a familial one. When Jack Lord joined in 1982 as a haulier, he found a company that seemed to be thoughtfully and efficiently run. Production shift workers had regular breaks from the noise and tedium of the job, and were so well taken care of that 'nobody ever left'. The Leicester factory, Jack said, was 'superb, like a hospital', organised and clean. There were hot meals in the canteens, pay rises, friendships. 'It was like a family. Nothing was too much.'

Jack's job interview consisted of a 'little drive around the base', to see if he was capable of driving an articulated vehicle. And then he was sent to be measured by the tailor, who would come to the factory on certain days, and who then went off to make him three bespoke dark blue Burton suits, to wear in the lorry cab. All delivery drivers got the tailor treatment for suits, plus three shirts, thermal underwear, thick boots, a Walkers tie and a weatherproof coat. 'The only thing they didn't give you was socks.' Walkers paid the laundry bill, too – part of the effort of making a good impression on the road, as the drivers unloaded the crisp pallets at clients' shops. 'Reputation and recommendation,' Jack said. 'You had a standard to keep.'

Routes in the early days took him around Manchester, and then later further afield to Lancashire and Norwich. 'We gradually expanded and needed more vehicles. Walkers wanted another influx of drivers.' By 1984, Britons were spending £805 million on crisps and snacks, or 0.3 per cent of national spending, according to Mintel research. At the end of the decade, annual spending on crisps in Britain surpassed the £1 billion mark.

And then things began to change. Walkers changed ownership from RJR Nabisco (which had merged with Standard Brands) with two quick successive sales to a French company and then a consortium. When PepsiCo took over in 1989, the mood was unsettled. 'We had good rapport, but it gradually got eroded,' Jack said. Management would say things like, 'We'll give you a rise but do away with the dinner money,' he recalled. 'We lost things to gain things.'

He knew something was firmly, irreversibly worse when Pepsi-Co got rid of the crisp drivers' Burton suits. In their place, the cab uniform turned into 'stupid overalls, and they didn't look right. The smartness was gone.' The vehicles themselves started to look shabbier, too – protocol used to be to wash them every time they arrived back at the depot, or drivers would face a hairdrying from the well-liked but potent transport foreman, Bill Bates. 'You had to do it. If you had done something wrong, you would get it.' The infamous 'Old Bill' would not approve of the private fleet that delivers Walkers crisps these days, according to Jack. 'He would be turning over to see the trailers now.'

Soon enough the canteen converted to vending machines, and the ration of a box of free crisps every Friday for the hauliers stopped, too, according to Jack, when it was suspected that the crisps were being resold on the black market. Instead drivers could fill a bin bag with what they liked for a fiver. 'The personal bit disappeared. You didn't know the bloke you were sitting next to in the canteen. You're now a number.'

The 1990s were a sharper-elbowed era for crisps. By 1992, Walkers had already received investment to create an automated warehouse, speeding up the last leg of the logistics to get crisps out of the door at pace. The previous twenty years had seen a flurry of buying, selling and subsuming of upstart, ailing busi-nesses in the British crisp landscape. The arrival of these potato chip powerhouse Americans was a definitive sign that a period of tough competition could now only intensify. Having boasted of the brand's humble beginnings in the 1961 corporate report, Frito-Lay's messaging was now more robust from the C-suites in Dallas. There was real money to be pursued in British crisps.

The big three – Smith's, Golden Wonder and Walkers – tried vehemently to outdo each other in the postwar market, which had grown in step with the strengthening network of the supermarkets. The new shopping arena was enabling the so-called 'crisp wars'.

we lost things to gain things

In 1958, the vast majority of British crisp consumption – some 75 per cent – took place in licensed premises. Grocers, newsagents and own-brand scraped together the rest of the sales. A decade later, in 1969, the trend had reversed, and only 25 per cent of sales were in the licensed trade, with the majority of the remainder falling to grocers.

All supermarkets and grocers were now showcases for brands, and for the imaginative limits of crisp and snack ideation. Smith's had answered Walkers' cheese and onion answer to Tayto's original cheese and onion flavour with the simple brilliance of salt and vinegar in 1966, redolent of the seasoning at the traditional fish and chip shop. Not only was it a good idea, but it was also pushed to the nation as a good idea by Smith's with a doubling in media advertising against the previous year, to a considerable £446,000 (about £7 million today).

Golden Wonder stepped up its flavour programme accordingly, but Smith's then came up with a £50 million hit in 1968 in the shape of a musical note, the potato-starch Quaver.

Golden Wonder returned to the fray with an equal smash in the form of Wotsits, and from there rode high in the crisp charts thanks to the frankly genius formulation of these fluffy, cheesy pellets. (Wotsits were the jewel of the management buyout of Golden Wonder in 1995, later sold to private equity in 2000 and then to another consortium in 2003, with Walkers buying the individual Wotsit brand the same year.)

Writing in the *Journal of Industrial Economics* in 1974, the academic Alan Bevan examined how such a significant shift had come about in the structure of the crisp industry: how British crisps had changed from being dominated by one major player – Smith's, fringed by an assortment of local hopefuls – to being a playing field with three equally threatening teams: Smith's, Golden Wonder and Walkers. Bevan identifies some key reasons for this change.

First, the equipment. In the 1950s, Smith's had been batch-cooking its crisps, a process that we would consider premium today, but which under early manufacturing techniques produced uneven results. The introduction of continuous frying machines from America solved this issue of consistency, and also ramped up the speed of potato-to-packet production. One continuous fryer could replace twenty batch cookers. Such equipment was expensive, but radical in effect.

Golden Wonder's owner, Imperial Tobacco, considered the investment worthwhile when it assumed control in 1961. Backing its new bet on diversification with cash, Imperial Tobacco built two Golden Wonder factories in England, and a third in Scotland. This meant that continuous frying equipment could be installed by design, and at speed, whereas Smith's had to lumber through plans for taking out old machines and rearranging their factory floors for new ones.

Form-fill-seal machinery, which displaced the previous system of individual pre-made crisp bags being delivered to crisp factories, also sped up the rate of genesis inside the factory. It created a ceaseless tube of packets, filled by automation with crisps and sealed with heat-sealing 'jaws'. The improved quality of the plastic bags, displacing wax glassine, in turn lengthened the shelf life of crisps from three days to up to six months. This generated a more favourable impression of Golden Wonder's freshness among customers, and repeat custom was primed to become a habit.

Walkers at this point was still relatively small – at the end of the 1960s, it had only 8 per cent market share. Smith's market share steadily declined throughout the decade, while Golden Wonder climbed, thanks in part to an advertising campaign that set its sights on national domination. Crisps were seen as 'old-fashioned, unglamorous', Bevan wrote, a challenge that was addressed through the new medium of household television audiences. By the middle of the 1960s, Golden Wonder was spending half a million pounds a year on advertising. Golden Wonder saw women as a new customer segment – men were the ones buying Smith's crisps in pubs, so they decided to leave that market alone and switch footing to the grocery stores. Crisps drifted upwards in layers of the public conversation, being chosen as the 'luxury' item by several of Roy Plomley's guests on *Desert Island Discs*, including by broadcaster David Frost, who in 1963 requested 'a vat of those potato crisps' for his marooned future.

In 1969, the oil in everyone's fryers cooled suddenly with the introduction of HMRC's purchase tax on crisps. The official reasoning, as described in Parliament, was to introduce a new suite of rates for correcting tax anomalies in modern British living: to catch taxation up with the way we lived now. It was deemed unjust, for example, that mattresses were subject to purchase tax, but knitting wool and textiles were not. This was changed. And so was the situation vis à vis potato crisps, per the Labour chancellor Roy Jenkins's speech:

> Confectionery, soft drinks and ice cream are now taxed at 22 per cent. I propose to extend this rate to potato crisps, as well as salted or roasted nuts. I also propose to bring prepared pet foods – widely advertised, no doubt appreciated, but not an essential means of feeding a pet – into tax at the same rate. These two groups, details of which are also set out in the Budget Report, are estimated to bring in an extra £22 million in a full year.

Though this measure was abolished in 1972, it was replaced by Denis Healey's Value Added Tax on crisps in 1974. A Commons debate went late into the night over whether this was the right thing to do. Michael Shersby, Conservative MP for Uxbridge, was concerned it was not:

'What about potato crisps, which are to bear the full rate of VAT? Many of my constituents find potato crisps a helpful, useful and convenient part of their diet. They eat them with salads and with other nutritious foods, but they will go up in price by 10 per cent.'

Pressures from all sides now made the crisp industry earn a reputation for being cut-throat. And in the middle of all this, Smith's had been caught off guard by a classic business mistake, Bevan concluded. It had felt reassured that sales were increasing, to record levels some years, but this blinded the company to the problem that its market share was shrinking. Walkers had increased its sales four-fold in the 1960s, while Smith's was still floundering, in spite of its acquisition of Tudor Crisps in 1960. Flavour and novelty became ever more important to success: what had started as small fry was not small fry any more. Crisps were in deep.

Someone, inside or outside the crisp factory, had to come up with the ideas. Take Thai sweet chilli in Walkers' noughties premium line, Sensations, for example. Every aspect of this flavour had been considered carefully. Flavourists had even been dispatched to a top restaurant in Bangkok to work with a chef, in order to nail the exact taste that should be carried on the crisp. It remains a top seller.

Flavour houses, meanwhile, had ringfenced teams working on different companies' products. But the issue of intellectual property – who owned which flavour, or whether anyone owned it at all – seems to have been unclear. Unlike a system of royalty payments derived from traditional IP, flavour seems to have worked along the lines of the implied equity that comes from an order of considerable size. So if you ordered thousands of tonnes of, say, cheese and cucumber flavouring, there was an understanding that it couldn't be made for anyone else. Purchasing power rather than legal agreements controlled the flavour arrangements. If you were ordering enough seasoning for a hundred million packets, for example, that was persuasive enough to stop the supplier from shipping it out to other buyers. But there was always the risk that an idea could be copied.

Each member of a crisp brand's family had to be continually improved or made over. Larry Bush joined the Walkers research and development team in 1996 at the peak of this experimental phase; an idealistic earth sciences graduate who had worked his first five professional years at Rio Tinto. Larry had visions of exploring places like Brazil and turning the mining conglomerate into a source for good, but instead got a terse industrial education on attachments to aluminium smelters in Anglesey and corrugated roofers in the West Midlands. 'It was, "Here's the world of work and here's how manufacturing works,"' he said cheerfully. These days, Larry runs a wildlife attraction near Bristol, and when we spoke he was taking a break from the zoo's playful Andean bears, the Peruvian inspiration for Paddington. 'It's a very outdoorsy life,' he added. 'Definitely not dull.'

Twenty-six-year-old Larry, disillusioned, answered a job ad for PepsiCo, and found himself interviewed at Walkers by managers who were also very young but 'quite nice people. The atmosphere was, "We mean business, we'll go for it," but in a naturally competitive way.' And, of course, 'We all liked crisps – someone would knock on the door and say, "Try these roast beef Monster Munch." It was really fun.' (Jack Lord, too, remembered women wandering the Leicester factory with trays of new crisps to try.)

The R&D department had a mandate to eat crisps endlessly, opening all the unbranded silver bags that came from wild flavour experiments, most of which never made it onto the market. At Christmas, staff were given a bonus in the form of a forty-eight-packet box of crisps in the flavours of their choice. People would go splits with friends and divide the ration between their favourite flavours, Larry said.

Working at crisp headquarters during this time was also cosmopolitan. In R&D the British team had colleagues in Poland, the US, Russia and Turkey, and worked very closely with people in Mexico, where PepsiCo had large market share. It was, Larry said, 'a stimulating environment: the culture was very international and youthful'.

The new American owners had influenced this culture, but they had sharp ideas too. They wanted to push Walkers' market share forward by introducing snack styles that already flew off the shelves in the US. In particular, they wanted the UK to fall in love with Doritos tortilla chips, which had launched in 1994. Larry was duly assigned to a special Doritos project team, a group seen as 'maverick' at the time, somewhat outsiders to the traditional Walkers team.

The brief appeared simple: make Doritos a bestseller. Tortilla-style chips had already become a business proposition in 1980s Britain through the Phileas Fogg brand of Derwent Foods, a premium 'posh' brand, buoyed by the clever marketing of the eponymous moustache-twirling adventurer Phileas Fogg. (I still remember the airmail envelope trim to the packets, and the dry, almost uncannily evenly spaced toasted spots of those Phileas Fogg tortilla triangles, flat with just-curled tips and thick-cut with an unthreatening but pleasant chilli heat. I liked them, but they were as nothing in my affections compared with Phileas Fogg's oil-baked garlic crouton Mignons Morceaux, which were the subject of some of our most furious family arguments.) Doritos were an 'incredible success' from the start, Larry said, but not quite incredible enough by PepsiCo standards.

Though Walkers had its offices at Theale, some of the Doritos mavericks were moved to an old warehouse on the outskirts of Leicester, not unlike one of the rustier manufacturing outfits where Larry had worked at Rio Tinto. 'Give them this annexe and see how it works out' was the thinking for the assignment, he said. They were aware of 'huge expectations', but most of these landed on the then president of Walkers, Martin Glenn, who was under 'incredible pressure', Larry said, from colleagues Stateside to make Doritos work.

What's interesting about this is the scale of the ambition that was conveyed across the Atlantic. 'The expectation from the US was that Doritos should be bigger than Walkers,' Larry said. In other words, tortilla chips should eclipse potato crisps. 'Ridiculously ambitious. We knew that was ridiculous. In reality what happened was we were aiming for the moon but got a third of the way there. Doritos were massive, but it was nowhere near the Americans' expectations.'

Even with launch marketing budgets for Doritos in the tens of millions, the crisp was still mightier in Britain than the tortilla. And the Americans were perplexed. They had failed to understand, Larry felt, that tortillas are popular in the US because Mexico is just 'over the border' – that tastes and cultures are porous and reactive to the closest contrasts.

Yet after internal review, the PepsiCo team decided that the problem must in fact lie in British production faults. 'The thinking from America was, "You're just not making them right. Send your guys over and we'll show you what it's all about."'

Half a dozen people then went on an American tortilla road trip, flown from the Midlands to meet every last Doritos guru in the United States. They started at the so-called 'Pentagon of Snacks' at the Frito-Lay plant in Dallas, and went on to plants in Phoenix, Modesto and Salt Lake City. In each place they met an expert on how to manufacture or select the ingredients. 'What was impressive was the real obsession to make a good product. There is an integrity about that. Maybe we're taking it too seriously and it's just a crisp. But that culture has been key. We'd never produced what the Americans thought was the gold standard.'

In Amarillo the research group observed the maize being delivered and saw the buyers' finicky sifting and rejection of cracked corn. At the time, back home, Walkers was setting up Spanish and Greek maize supply chains, and 'we were accepting whatever was being grown. That trip influenced the agronomic programme.'

PepsiCo's tortillas begin with whole maize kernels soaked in kettles before milling and toasting. The group learned how the millstones affected the end product, and followed through with improvements back at the new Coventry factory for Doritos. They saw how the maize dough goes on to a sheeting belt and then into a toasting oven, whereupon the soft doughy triangles are fried to get their signature blisters. 'To get those right you have to get the milling right and the toasting right.'

By the time the Doritos researchers came back to the UK, they were understandably primed for tortilla craft obsession. 'We were in the Coventry factory day and night and we were like, "the oil is right, the mill is right", and it still wasn't gold.' They worked monomaniacally to improve the product until, finally, they got approval from America. Celebrations were held at the local TGI Fridays, in true 1990s style.

And yet. The research trip did not do what it was supposed to, inasmuch as it did not propel Doritos into the stratosphere. 'We did lift the quality of Doritos. But we didn't take it from a £50 million to a £500 million business.'

This is a curious problem for brands with perishable goods and global markets. How can you recreate, exactly, the standard and the taste of a well-known product in different locales? The ingredients, almost by necessity, cannot all be from the same source. It would be economically and environmentally perverse to ship all the required maize from America to Coventry. Ultimately, companies rely on branding to convince consumers that they're eating the same Doritos in Modesto as they are in Manchester. Consumers become the bridge between all the tiny differences in the thousands of miles between.

Meanwhile, on the subject of standardisation, the Americans had a new idea. PepsiCo wanted to create one global nation of snacks. One big brand. Why not push, PepsiCo argued, to simply get rid of Walkers and make everything Lay's?

This notion, which was reputedly debated off and on from the late nineties to early noughties, did not go down well at Walkers.

we lost things to gain things

There was a 'big battle', Larry said. Walkers Crisps was a product of wartime resilience, of perseverance, of the (once-) great British talent for organisation. If the name Walkers was removed, it would signal a rent in the fabric of post-war brands that had settled into successive generations' shopping baskets. No matter that the product had changed, there was reassuring continuity in the name.

> We felt it was crazy – and an affront to our heritage. There was a real 'defender of the brand' move from Walkers. Walkers are really good at understanding that you're creating something that's enjoyable and gives people a lift. We used to have a mantra there of 'food for feelings' and simple pleasures. There's a lot of nostalgia and cultural affinity for crisps.

He goes further. 'You could put people into crisp tribes depending on where you grew up. Crisps are almost like a member of the family.'

And though the counties of Britain can map out crisp flavour preferences and brand loyalties, they are unified by a shared taste for a deadpan outlook. 'The unique ingredient in Britain is a shared sense of humour. I don't think there is that anywhere else in the world. Walkers really tapped into it.'

8

salt and lineker

When I was a child, I started collecting paper bags. It began with the *boulangeries* and *traiteurs* in Brittany and Normandy, on our 1980s series of campsite and gîte holidays. The bakeries printed their addresses on white paper in curls of red and navy serifs, and they twisted baguettes and brioches up in sheets patterned with sepia-drawn ears of wheat and bow-wrapped cakes, among which promises were printed. 'Les Français fabriquent le meilleur pain'. 'Saveur et finesse des friandises'. 'Un raffinement dans l'art d'offrir'.

When I understood the French words I also believed them, since nothing I ate contradicted the boasting. The French clearly did make the best bread. A truth to keep and cherish. (I read these slogans from *boulangerie* papers I stuck into my diary at the time, which I still have.)

Over a few years my collection grew to encompass any paper bag that featured attractive typography and/or some nominal memento value, or an interesting shape. I jealously kept this stash of paper under the bed, as if a burglar might otherwise head straight for it. So believe me when I say that, as an adult, I very much have a favourite plastic bag.

No surprise, it is a crisp-related carrier. Issued in 2019 by Sainsbury's in the 1980s design of its multipack crisps, it is a 'bag for life' blessed with sturdy handles and thick, crinkled plastic. When I saw it, I was struck immediately by shopper's haste. As quickly as possible, this must become mine.

These days, it looks a little careworn. But its message is undimmed. The orange and yellow diagonal slashes of 1980s colour, the bubbled lettering spelling out 'POTATO CRISPS', even the straight sans-serif Sainsbury's name, all create a sense of timelessness. It is a piece of the past that can carry things and be lifted at the same time, above the difficulty of reality at ground level.

These were the very packets that featured in my repertoire of crisp-shrinking at home – own-brand crisps shrunk next to teensy Scampi Fries and Walkers prawn cocktail, as if to make an imperfectly shrivelled corner shop. Even the distinct fruit-squash colouring of the old Sainsbury's branding reads to me as instantly nostalgic, like the opening chord of an old pop song.

Both a container for a quick snack, and themselves a durable piece of engineering, crisp packets embody a contradiction. Most take around eighty years to decompose, equal to a human lifetime. This fact, and the lack of recycling possibilities, became the prompt for the Crisp Packet Project (CPP) in Hastings, East Sussex, where groups of volunteers use donations of crisp packets to sew kits for the homeless. This isn't a characteristic of crisp packets that I had considered before, or really that anyone should be forced by necessity to consider – that they are naturally reflective and waterproof, and so suitable material for an emergency blanket. CPP now has chapters around the country, fashioning wash bags, pillows and sleeping bags that each require a full four metres square of empty plastic, around forty-four packets in total per crisp cocoon. More recently, and even more bleakly, the project has started sending crisp-packet blankets into war zones.

Holding on to used crisp packets in private, and not for public benevolence, might, however, be interpreted as subversive – as if not letting go is holding back the correct order of consumption and disposal, of enjoying and forgetting, of moving forward. Why hold on to something, if its original purpose has expired? De La Warr Pavilion gallery in Bexhill-on-Sea, East Sussex, hosted an exhibition in 2010 of crisp packets in its regular Collectors Corner, showcasing the 250-strong selection amassed in the 1980s by a local man, Dave Valentine. At the time, the collection was valued at £10,000 for its rarity. The exhibition drew a good crowd, and provoked much debate, De La Warr said, over the graphics and tastes of displayed snacks such as Burger Bites, Ringos, Wheat Crunchies, Discos, Piccolos and Crunchy Waffles. Dave was a small boy when he focused on the collection, encouraged by his family to pursue his crisp-packet curation as an alternative to watching too much television. There was considerable excitement in the press about the startling value of the collection, and an implicit respect for the fact he had bothered at all, where no one else had.

The exhibition captured the visual specificity that the members of each crisp generation attach to their wistfulness. Even more potent, perhaps, is the realm of discontinued flavours and lost brands, whose tangible legacy is limited to the packet design. Oxo-flavoured crisps by the Chipmunk brand, for example, were by all accounts quick trade in school tuck shops in the 1960s, boasting a mythically tangy beef and onion kick that fans have not forgotten. But all I can do today is guess at the taste from the packet.

Flat crisp packets are not the loveliest sight. Once void of fried potatoes, they seem to undergo an instant and drastic ageing process, as if they have in fact been crumpled by years of uselessness without their crisps to carry. It makes me think of the British designer Anya Hindmarch's tribute to the unopened crisp packet in handbag form – a shiny metallic fabric cast of the shape, contoured with folds to suggest a complete bag of crisps inside. Made in Italy, lined in suede, the Crisp Packet Clutch costs a cool £1,600. The absurdity of the price is part of the product, a feature of most designer handbags, but with the difference here that the joke is clearly shared. In the pun on something that should be throwaway, there's also an artistry in the way that this bag demands careful ownership – to stay intact, to never be scratched, to be forever expectant with folds of gold coins.

That 'lost British crisps' have a secondary market value is another fact that convinces me the British take crisps more seriously than other nations. Somewhere, scrolling through eBay, there appear to exist crisp completists who combine the mysterious combination of spare cash and fandom serious enough that they will start bidding on desiccated potatoes.

'I'm selling as a collectible item and am warning no one to eat any of the crisps inside for obvious reasons.' So writes one eBay user about their listing of a single packet of ten-year-old, discontinued Worcestershire sauce crisps, a tart flavour I personally lament the passing of, though I wouldn't pay the asking price here of £250. If winters in Glasgow did not make my flat as cold as a well (to paraphrase the best description of Scottish cold from

R. L. Stevenson's *Kidnapped*) and expensive to heat, I might consider a maximum bid of, say, £25.

This is by no means the only 'vintage' crisp listing on eBay, and nor is it the only one to exhibit apparent insanity or wishful thinking, possibly both. At the time of writing you can also bid for a packet of limited edition chilli and chocolate Walkers crisps (expiry date 23.05.09) for £500.

But what is madder, £500 on a packet of crisps that cannot be eaten, or a lifetime of crisps that adds up to thousands of pounds, and counting? I had a similar reckoning when I left London and realised I had spent *a lot* of money at Pret a Manger. Had it been worth it? I wondered. Yes, I eventually decided, and yes for my crisp thousands too. The money spent accrues, but the comfort of a good lunch or a quick crisp does not; it has to be reset each time, in step with the body's daily resetting of hunger. Each lunch, and every crisp, has some new bond to make.

Though graphic design has always helped to sell products, for crisps I think it has never been able to exceed the importance of the contents inside. To create loyalty among childhood consumers, branding did not necessarily need to be brilliant, but in some dimension it had to be accurate. If it made promises or impressions, they had to be followed through. The multipack branding was equal to its contents: nothing fancy, nothing unacceptable. Small, portable bags of crisps fitted neatly into children's lunchboxes, but more importantly they appealed to their unlimited appreciation of stranger things – of crisps that were at heart based on crazy ideas. The snaggle-toothed monster of Monster Munch packets was just wild enough, and to my knowledge it has never been redrawn. The picture matches the sour furry taste of the munchies exactly.

In this sense, crisps were a canvas for early connoisseurship, a field that could be fully surveyed and weighed up. It was a chance, long before the arrival of adulthood, to be certain of your own opinions. Tokens on the back of packets also dangled the possibility of collecting a small but satisfying junk shop's worth of prizes. Crispi Crisps, in the early 1970s, went so far as to produce a full catalogue of gifts that could be exchanged against its crisp coupons, ranging from a Thermos picnic set to a dartboard, a garden trowel and a box of dominoes.

I remember the special thrill of this kind of coupon correspondence with big unseen companies in faraway cities, marvelling at how generously they might exchange gifts with you and send them to your house, regardless of how far down an overgrown lane it happened to be. When a free gift arrived at the door after months of careful coupon collection, it felt like an endorsement of your very being. This lifeline extended across cereal boxes, football stickers and junior bank accounts. All you had to do was keep buying and eating.

This idea – that the crisp packet could be a portal to another world – was mirrored in the Tayto Park in County Meath, Ireland, a zoo and amusement park where your entry ticket got you a free packet of crisps. The Meath park was the brainchild of 'Ireland's crisp king', Raymond Coyle, who started the Irish crisp brand Hunky Dorys and for a time owned Tayto and King Crisps as part of Largo Foods. He was inspired, as his *Irish Times* obituary stated, by how Milton Hershey, 'owner of the world's first chocolate factory, had built Hershey Park in Pennsylvania, initially as a place for his employees and their families to relax and later a big tourist attraction'.

In 2022, when the Irish snack company's headline sponsorship finished, the hybrid theme park rebranded as Emerald Park and, to much sadness, no longer distributes free Tayto crisps to ticket holders. (Job ads for Tayto itself still list free canteen crisps among the perks, however.)

In other European countries, such a park might not have the emotional motive to exist – crisp culture doesn't extend as much there. One of Larry Bush's theories for this gap in caring is that in the 1970s and 1980s, the UK at least simply didn't have a culturally rich landscape. 'Maybe crisps were our cultural wealth. In France and Spain, why would you bother? In America they do care more deeply. But they're not as eccentric.'

There is also the common understanding between manufacturer and consumer in British crisp culture, a bond of long-running humour that makes crisps a bit like a never-ending soap opera, with changing characters and some original cast members who will apparently live forever.

All this played into the comfortable invisibility of the people who actually made the product. If you tried to name the CEO of a crisp company of any era, you would be destined to fail – other than 'Mr Smith' or 'Mr Walker', which would only get you half a pub-quiz point. As potatoes grow underground, so crispers like to stay inside the factory, resolutely faceless. The business is the brand, the brand the business. People sitting at the board table are visually irrelevant to marketing success. Farmers, in place of crispers, are more likely to become the poster faces for the product via the wholesome leverage of potato-rearing.

At a stretch, the pre- or post-war founder of the business can make an appealing figurehead, captured in a photograph where the future success of the enterprise is unwritten, impossible even, given its modest setting. Salvador Bonilla, for example, printed in black and white, stares back at the photographer from a motorbike lashed with crisp tins in Galicia, *circa* 1950. Bonilla is unusual for continuing to be run as a family business, since the late César Bonilla, Salvador's son, continued to helm the show into his nineties. Usually, these 'before' photos are a natural point of pride that celebrates business growth, but the 'after' is so often faceless.

Indeed, if you had heard of a crisp company CEO, it would be because they had committed a sin or a considerable error. There is no Whitney Wolfe, James Dyson or Steve Jobs of crisps: no one who has proclaimed an epoch-making disruption to the old ways, as the above trio did for dating, hand-drying and computing. Potatoes are potatoes.

The closest icon available is Mr Tayto, a spud in a red jacket who fronts the Irish and Northern Irish companies that take his name.

Mr Tayto is famous on the Emerald Isle. He has fans, even romantic admirers, and a respectable following for his own Instagram account. Though his yellow potato-bellied likeness is as familiar as a shamrock in Ireland, a very fond cliché, it is protected as intellectual copyright – you can't be guaranteed to hire a Mr Tayto suit from a fancy-dress shop. He had to be booked to appear at the opening night of the Eatyard Crisp Festival in Dublin, and is accustomed to having photographs taken with politicians. In 2009, he wrote a fictionalised account of his life, published in Ireland as *The Man Inside the Jacket*. (Page 1: 'Every Irish fella thinks they've got a book in them . . .')

When it comes to crisps and advertising, there is an art of frying lightly. A friendly or cheeky or irreproachable face seems to be an ideal pitch for selling crisps – a way of implying that innocence will be the first thing that hits you when you open up a packet.

Crisp companies established this idea of harmless fun cleverly, but then started to undermine themselves with the use of advertising slogans. Post-war Walkers briefly printed 'Any time is opening time' on its packets as a slightly acidic joke about crisps and boozers. In the 1960s, it also ran a TV ad featuring a cockney 'robber' breaking into the factory and filling a poacher's jacket with crisp packets before being caught by a policeman. 'Well, with so many flavours, can you resist?' was his defence.

Golden Wonder, ramping up its ad spend in the 1960s under Imperial Tobacco's ownership, came up with the tagline 'You could eat a million, and still want more', which is a tidy if slightly cruel summation of the consumer experience.

crunch

KP had a sweet TV campaign in a cartoon animation *circa* 1979, featuring an interview at a monastery for a wannabe 'KP fryer' (a good pun). The aspiring friar/fryer tastes the crisps and declares them 'Truly, a crisp among crisps', which is then adopted as the monks' business slogan. Tudor Crisps focused on its regional audience with a Geordie paper boy taking packets from the newsagents out of his wages, and then tricking a small boy into delivering a paper in a block with no working lift, all in exchange for crisps.

Director Paul Weiland in 1980 shifted into a more original and modern tone with his psychedelic campaign for Smith's Squares, featuring a young Lenny Henry (Slogan: 'Eating is believing').

Walkers' campaigns with footballer Gary Lineker, or more recently with celebrity cook Nigella Lawson, have strived to maintain crisps' role as an adjunct to British humour. Gary Lineker, formerly the England team's striker, was an ideal candidate, not least because he hailed from Leicester, where the crisps are made.

Lineker's first piece of work with Walkers, the so-called 'welcome home' ad, was a spoof on Lineker's niceness. He is shown returning to Leicester from a stint playing in Japan and amiably greeting his fans, but then steals a packet of cheese and onion from a boy sitting on a park bench. A sportsman cheekily endorsing crisps didn't seem to rouse health concerns. When Gary Lineker's 'welcome home' ads first ran, the thing people called in to the Independent Television Commission to complain about was the meanness of his behaviour towards the little boy.

Paul Weiland had directed episodes of *Mr Bean* and had just the right grasp on British tolerance for self-congratulation and self-deprecation. He returned to Walkers for a follow-on ad for 'salt and Lineker', a re-faced salt and vinegar edition that again featured Lineker being uncharacteristically mean, crunching away on a packet of the 'new flavour' in a football stand, and then crushing the fingers of Paul Gascoigne in the stands behind him when he tries to poach a few crisps.

Lineker went on to be the long-running crisp frontman for Walkers, a perfect specimen of health and achievement who had a knack of making crisp eating look like good, clean fun.

Later, as Walkers manoeuvred the campaign in 2006 to reposition its product as improved on health merits, it produced a poster that equated its salt content with a slice of white bread. Gary Lineker was depicted holding a packet of ready salted crisps in one hand and a slice of bread in the other. The poster text read: 'There's now as little salt in here . . . as there is in here.' The lobby group Consensus Action on Salt and Health complained to the Advertising Standards Agency that this comparison was misleading, but its complaint was not upheld.

Such complaints were invariably dismissed on the grounds of reasonable interpretation. Would anyone really rush out to buy more crisps, thinking they were as nutritious as a slice of bread? Probably not. And would anyone really be influenced by Lineker's jokey bad example to children and former teammates? The weight of probability and the assumption of common sense protected these advertisements from the more abstract effect they had on consumers. They made light of crisps as a habit-forming diet.

Pringles' 'Once you pop, you can't stop' slogan in 1996 set the bar much higher for all players in the snack category. Created by an agency collaboration between Zambrelli and Wells Rich Greene, it was at once lethally accurate and a universally magnetic instruction. And again, it was accurate: I have never experienced anything less than a struggle to prevent myself from eating an entire tube of Pringles in one sitting. This remains, by some margin, the best and perhaps the only great advertising slogan to have been conceived for the potato-chip market. Pringles has since dialled down the mood of uncontrolled dietary destiny, which is off-key in the health-aware age, and replaced it with the far tamer statement of 'Mind-popping'.

Contrast this with Sweden, where the popular trend for *fredagsmys*, or 'cosy Friday', has oriented crisp marketing in the same wholesome direction. *Fredagsmys* is a reflection of the Swedish observance of hard-working weeks and self-improving midweek evenings of sport and hobbies, with relaxation scheduled nationwide at 5 p.m. on Fridays. Mexican food has been enduringly fashionable in Sweden since the 1990s, and tacos and tortillas are a staple of *fredagsmys* dinners. The word itself was popularised in the 1990s by Swedish crisp brand OLW, which had the slogan 'On Fridays we do *fredagsmys*' and a matching, hymnal song. Obesity rates have increased slowly but steadily in Sweden in the past forty years, but still compare favourably with other OECD countries.

In England, 1980, a year after I was born, 6 per cent of adults were classified as obese. In 2020, the proportion had risen to 24.8 per cent. A report in the *British Medical Journal* in 2017 reported that 'Spending on junk food advertising is nearly 30 times what government spends on promoting healthy eating'. Subsequent consultation advanced the regulation of 'HFSS' (high in fat, salt or sugar) ads that stood any chance of being seen by children, introducing a 9 p.m. watershed across TV and on-demand services. The problem this tackles is stark. More than one in five children in England are obese or overweight by the time they start primary school, the Department of Health noted, and this rises to more than one-third by the time they leave. Two-thirds of British adults are above a healthy weight. (Though I have never been a waif, I walk a lot, and sometimes run a lot, so my crisp habit is not necessarily reflected in my size.)

Advertising supported – even taunted – consumers into believing that the products they sold were irresistible. It also created an anticipation, when you shopped, that the purchase itself was what was hard to resist, not the product. The consumable things that I remember from the 1990s all huddle around branding that was tantalisingly out of reach. I longed for stops at the Little Chefs on motorways. I knew that McCain crinkle-cut chips were the chips we should be eating with breaded scampi, not supermarket own-branded. The same rule applied to ice cream. The Viennetta log of chocolate-layered vanilla was a 'posh' treat, but even the closest imitators were not.

For parents, crisps were also good babysitters. In the Northern Ireland Community oral archive, Nigel Flynn, who grew up in Ballymena in the 1970s, recalled how his grandfather had seen alcohol as the 'devil's buttermilk', but his father was fond of a drink – and of pubs. And so Nigel was given a packet of crisps and orange mineral while his father went inside his local for a beer. 'You sit in the car while I just go and have one,' he used to say.

There was this other side to all 'junk' food, a doubt that would sometimes shadow enjoyment. In 2005, the National Consumer Council (NCC) commissioned a 'Shopping Generation' survey of ten-to-nineteen-year-old children, the first comprehensive study of its kind in the UK, and it revealed anxiety behind the children's purchasing power.

At this point under-sixteens were already collectively spending £680 million of their own pocket money every year on snacks. The overall market for 'child-oriented' consumption was worth around £30 billion. Yet the report found the children felt a pressure to consume, and an exposure to invasive advertising. There was also 'an aspiration gap' in disadvantaged households between what was advertised and what was affordable, and a sense that children were being 'ripped off' by promotions and false expectations. British children, the report also noted, were 'more brand-aware, more receptive to adverts and less happy with what they had to spend' when compared with their American counterparts.

The US data came from Juliet B. Schor's book *Born to Buy: The Commercialized Child and the New Consumer Culture*. Schor noted how quick industry was to point out that both children and their parents were at liberty to say no to junk food, when a systematic lobby for high-fat, high-salt, high-sugar retail in fact made this refusal impracticable. Some states even had been lobbied to pass disparagement laws making it illegal to make certain statements about food, Schor noted. That parents might have the agency to intervene overlooked the fact that they were pressured on other fronts to control what their children consumed – from television to gaming to music lyrics. 'Food is a tough battle in the midst of other influences that seem more immediate and pernicious,' Schor wrote. Parents found it easiest to cede ground on food, and keep their powder dry for bigger battles.

In 2006, the year after the NCC report was published, British children went back to school after the summer holidays with a few things missing from the vending machines. The government's new food-based standards for school lunches banned all crisps from the food available within school walls. 'Savoury snacks such as crisps should not be available for lunch. Only nuts and seeds with no added salt, sugar or fat are allowed.' Public-sector food procurement was also rethought more broadly, meaning crisps were no longer a daily feature at some of Her Majesty's prisons.

The NHS, too, as the UK's largest employer, was subject to a review of snack-food availability. In 2015, its vending machines dispensed 922.2 million products, ranging from snacks to cold drinks. The same year, the Department of Health carried out a trial in partnership with Selecta UK, a large vending machine operator, to see if product placement affected healthy choices in hospitals. Focused on the Leeds Teaching Hospitals NHS Trust, the experiment phased out the presence of branded crisps in six vending machines and gradually made healthier choices such as nuts and fruit more prominent.

It didn't lead to an avalanche of apples falling off the vending spirals. Instead, the decreased presence of branded crisps seemed to generate a switch to confectionery. 'The findings suggest that consumers switched their purchasing from crisps to confectionery (and to a lesser extent dried fruit and nut and other snacks). As the average total sugar content is substantially lower in crisps than confectionery, dried fruit and nuts and other snacks, we observe an increase in the total sugar.'

I think this tallies with my own experience with foods that teeter towards being vices. If I manage to suppress the appetite for one, another comes to replace it. Studies of 'food deserts' where supermarkets are unavailable or hard to reach have also pointed to complex behavioural patterns. A recent Government Office for Science review of obesogenic environments – the factors of price, availability, transport and built environment that may promote obesity – cited evidence that age, gender and cultural factors influenced fruit and vegetable intake rather than distance to fresh-food supermarkets.

Selecta now has a 'Mars Intelligent Vending Machine' that uses a digital touchscreen interface to shuffle suggestions. (It has not been placed in NHS environments to date, but in traditional on-street locations.) The fixed prominence of one snack over another is no longer relevant: the machine uses artificial intelligence and facial recognition to make a judgement call about what kind of snack personage stands in front of it. I wonder if it would see me and shuffle the crisps.

When someone walks into Atul Sodha's shop, he watches for which direction they will take. In shop-floor plans, there are 'hot paths' where premium branded merchandise instantly meets eyeballs and cooler paths where lower-margin stock is placed more discreetly. In the hot paths, the designs and slogans are intended to be irresistible.

Atul owns a Londis grocery store in Harefield, serving a village of about eight thousand people on the north-western outskirts of Greater London. In 1989, aged seventeen, he left school and started working: 'I didn't do too much academically,' he said wryly. The Sodha family had fled from Uganda to England in the 1970s, summarily exiled as Asians by President Idi Amin. Atul's mother, parenting alone, worked in a factory at first, and later took over her sister's convenience store.

Early in his working life, teenage Atul used to do evening shifts for an uncle who ran an off licence on a council estate. His uncle served the alcohol, and Atul served the dry goods. One customer, he remembered, had very specific taste in crisps.

'This lady used to come in at a particular time, every evening. She always bought prawn cocktail crisps, but she had to have them with a Topic – no other chocolate bar would do – and a can of Lilt.'

Eventually, passing this trio over the counter time and again made him curious. He wanted to know what the prawn–chocolate–pineapple ritual tasted like. 'I tried that same mix,' he recalled, 'and it triggered something in my taste buds.'

The experience made him consider how crisps can be 'anything to anyone'. At home his mother would use them to make an improvised Bombay mix, he said, by combining packets of ready salted and French Fries with nuts and spices. 'Snacking is such a huge thing in this country.'

Huge in both senses: snacking is hugely popular, and it is hugely personal, too. Every snacker adopts their own strange rituals. An old desk neighbour of mine at work would not open a packet of crisps unless his shirt sleeves covered his fingers. Some people like to smash the unopened packet down deliberately before opening, to enjoy a bag of potato splinters. There is a different kind of crisp love for every eater. American kettle-chip maker Boulder Canyon put a textural dimension of this to a vote on social media, asking whether people preferred to happen upon folded crisps, bubbles or crispy edges. (I think, like the majority of their respondents, I am #teamfolded, personally, for the double-crunch value.)

Today, Atul Sodha has a 650-square-foot store to fill. His supplier – and the fascia above the door – is Londis, owned by Tesco, and through them he gets three big deliveries a week – ambient, grocery and fresh – as well as dailies from local suppliers. Cash and carry is a back-up.

'Everything is about margin. The goods get delivered to Londis's warehouses by the brands, and based on that I chose to make my life easier and get the products delivered to my door. But there is a cost in having the stuff delivered.'

Grocers measure the importance of their stock displays not in units of goods but in linear meterage – literally, how much selling space an item or category takes up on the shop floor. Atul is 'more than over-indexed for crisps', he says, 'for the size of my store'. At his Harefield Londis, crisps are stocked along ten linear metres. KP, for whom he is a brand ambassador, also gave him a free-standing display unit at one point, but he used it instead as a cricket wicket.

The crisps arrive weekly, anywhere from twenty-five to fifty boxes of them, strapped into cages in delivery vans to protect the integrity of the product. He mentioned opening that morning's delivery and finding popped bags of Doritos – more paperwork to fill for the refund claim.

Sales-point data, crunched into different insights, informs Atul and other shop managers like him about what is performing well, at what point of the day and week, and flashes up anything that is languishing and needs to be rethought. 'I couldn't run my store with just a cash register.'

With or without data insights, one thing is certain: the British public love a promotion, and there will be spikes in sales on promo days. Christmas is another crisp peak, although this has levelled off since the permanent introduction of big sharing-bag sizes, which in the 1980s were only made available for Yuletide feasting.

For the margin, he is generally striving for a 30 per cent minimum – '50 per cent, you'd be doing well'. And if '£1.25 is the new £1', as he describes average pricing of a crisp packet, that means he is taking home about 37.5 pence for a sale, before other costs. To make crisps work, as is by now abundantly clear, they have to sell quickly, and in large quantities.

This is where shopkeeping becomes an art form. Being behind the counter is not just being on the receiving side of a transaction. The feelings of the social interactions are completely altered. Perceptions of what people have come into the shop for, and why, are important to understanding the performance of the business itself. 'We're looking at people's "mission" for why they come in,' as Atul said.

Weather changes shopping moods, but so do proximities. Every customer knows this when they see crisps waiting expectantly next to alcohol. This is just one aspect of the shop planogram, a spatial and scientific approach to optimisation of spending orchestrated by the retailer. It sounds calculated, and it is. Its power is now being curbed by 'HFSS' regulations that will alter what retailers can place where when promoting prices. Planogrammatic placements of high-fat, high-salt and high-sugar foods in parts of the customer journey where weakness might strike – at the till being the classic one – will be curtailed, although this will hit the supermarkets harder than the corner shops. (The regulations apply to stores larger than two thousand square feet and with fifty or more employees.)

For all grocery stores, profit comes from the right assembly of temptations. When Atul took over the Harefield store, it was a traditional confectionery, tobacco and news outlet, but he wanted to add groceries in order to attract more customers. He works on a basket spend in his store, and 'the only way to increase that is getting relevant things people want in their basket'.

Years ago he used CCTV footage to analyse the 'hot paths' of where people headed first when they came through the door. A customer who happened to work at Walkers Crisps had mentioned to him one day that the majority of people look left when they come into a shop. 'He said, "Have you thought about storing cheese and onion crisps there?" He was trying to prove a point to me.'

The pillars of the KP planogram, Atul said, are to display McCoy's first as a premium product, and then to fit in space for local flavours according to the demographic. 'Eighty per cent of the sales come from the twenty top lines. That's relevant to any category. People will come in for the iconic and heritage lines.'

Brand recognition enables quick decision-making. This is important since people don't want to spend a lot of time on grocery shopping. As discussed, it was one of the reasons that the traditional counter-service stores were phased out in the 1950s. When people had commutes and office jobs to worry about, and women began to join the workforce in increasing numbers, the last thing they wanted was to stand in line for a pound of flour. Within the new environment of self-service supermarkets, there was a fresh round of commercial opportunity: their own brand.

The late Joe Coulombe, founder of the upscale American food store Trader Joe's, took a particularly characterful approach to the potential for own-brand goods. Here was a man who was good at marketing, cynically and brilliantly so. He could sense, with gleeful accuracy, how the pitch of the dialogue between the branding in store and the customer's way of thinking could make the difference between a good day's and an average day's takings.

In his memoir *Becoming Trader Joe*, he writes of the importance of 'individualized labels aimed at the overeducated', such as Brandenburg Brownies, Peanut Pascal and Habeas Crispus potato chips, flattering the educational attainment of his customers. Though these were in-house products, the punning names were an attempt to differentiate from a 'one-size-fits-all private label like the supermarkets'. Wherever he could, Coulombe wrote, he used cultural references in the product names. 'Oh, we did had [sic] fun!'

Coulombe even admitted to selling factory sweepings of coffee beans under the name Heisenberg's Uncertain Blend. Revenue followed fun, because 'confidence in one product led to purchases of another'. The silliness didn't offend the customers, since they were privy to the joke.

In the 1930s, Waitrose's co-founder Wallace Waite used to ask his family for ideas for Waitrose own-brand names over Sunday lunch. Waitrose brands such as Sunny Brook and Round Tower were well designed and colourful, a good way to enliven ordinary cupboard staples such as sultanas.

Like Atul Sodha's small store, Waitrose had begun as a modest affair in Acton, London at the turn of the twentieth century. It had grown as the middle-class neighbourhood had grown, and strengthened itself early on through the adroit practice of commercial partnership.

Waitrose remains one of the smaller supermarket chains by turnover and number of branches, and it now keeps things frill-free in the design and marketing of its own brands. Rather than ascribing them character names, they speak of different financial imperatives – No. 1, for example, for the 1 per cent, or Essential, for the just-about-managing-to-shop-at-Waitrose within Waitrose's customer base.

Crisps, in all supermarkets, sell themselves. But to avoid sales cannibalisation between crisp brands, supermarkets are very picky about which lines they stock alongside their own brand. Sometimes this means favouring those who in fact make crisps on their behalf. In turn, this can mean that shelves of crisps along the straight line of the aisle are a parallel echo of the production line of a single factory. As so often in the world of crisps, an abundance of products doesn't necessarily mean an abundance of producers.

9

pickled fish

C asino Supermarché is a dangerous place for me to shop. For a few days over the summer, I went to Paris to work alone on some writing. And, apparently, I unconsciously had plans to eat a lot of cheese. It called out to me from the Casino fromage fridges, of which there are several in distinct spending areas, all cheese budgets catered for.

Compared with sterling prices, euro cheese is excellent value. Even a pre-packaged cheese board – Cantal to blues – was amazingly cheap, at about six euros. I imagined the baguette and cornichons and salami that I would get to go with it, and I could feel my childhood religious conversion to French food seeping back into my spirits.

I used to visit this same supermarket when I lived and worked in Paris for a few years in my early twenties. I remember the things I had *petites faiblesses* for then – the *pains au lait* and pre-rolled pancakes were a weekly must-have, the butter semi-salted from Normandy similarly essential, and the quartet packs of crème brûlée, cream-topped chocolate mousse and crème caramel tantalising for their gold foil lids and glass pots containing subtly different grades of indulgence.

Our office *déjeuner* breaks, meanwhile, mostly scorned packed lunches – we scouted instead the local restaurants around the Bastille for *prix-fixe* deals under twenty euros. Here were bistro bargains made for busy service: rillettes on toast, *brandade de morue* with whipped potatoes, and slices of *fondant au chocolat* with a quenelle of cream, washed down with *noisette* espressos, some of which could be exchanged for *tickets de restaurant* lunch vouchers. After work, we picked up where we had left off on the restaurant terraces, drinking kirs and wines from short, chilled glasses. Occasionally, in this *apéro* setting, a thimble ramekin of warm salty crisps would be served wordlessly with white wine. Never flavoured, always salted. Never asked for, always just democratically there, the final item from the waiter's tray, deposited like a quiet crisp punctuation mark on the table. Never more than about eight or nine crisps in the bowl. A few mouthfuls' worth. And that, it seems, was sufficient: it is the sum of my Parisian crisp memories.

Looking back, it makes sense to me that such an intense period of my life would be a crisp blank. Some cultures find a busyness of food to offer that utterly reframes crisps and relegates them sensibly to the sidelines. Italy is like this too, from my limited experience.

And so when I drifted round to the snacking aisle in Casino, twenty years later, there was a shock. The concept known in France as *l'art de vivre* – an understanding of living well – had at some point descended upon *la chip*. Where giant red mega-sacks of salted or chive or paprika crisps were what I expected to see, instead there were gourmet, regional, healthy variations, in a respectable assortment of shapes and sizes. They even had small, individual lunchbox packets (plus Lay's, of course).

Though I have been back and forth to Paris since living there, I think this was the first time that it really struck me how much shifting had taken place, and how little my own assumptions about France had changed in the same period. Les Brets, based in Brittany where I had first fallen for French crisps, is the national market leader in *la chip*, the first French company to create chips *aromatisées* with flavour. It came to life in the 1990s through a well-organised grower network of potato farmers in Brittany, and steadily increased its market share. When you consider the creativity of their flavours such as cherry and *brebis*, or *tartiflette*, it's a frustration to remember Brexit – how we probably won't be enjoying these thoughtful, quality crisps in British delis any time soon without a vinegary mark-up. Les Brets is an example of authentic flavours incorporated from raw goods, not matched in a lab, scaled to national distribution. Pipers is a British example of a similar but more limited approach, using Kirkby Malham chorizo, for example. But in my view at least, Les Brets are making far better crisps.

With this said, there is a complication. Though Les Brets has diversified into flavour with aplomb, as has Patatas Torres in Spain, there is a vein of European crisps that keeps things stubbornly simple. This is a personal understanding, rather than a market category, but I informally think of a certain kind of salted plain crisp as 'European', as if this itself were a local flavour.

Bonilla a la Vista, which started in Ferrol on Spain's northwestern coast in 1932, only makes plain sea-salted crisps, fried in cold-pressed virgin olive oil. It began as a *churros* and tortilla shop that also fried crisps, and later sold its products to guests at its hotel on the town's railway pier. Bonilla's main export market today is South Korea, where a boom in sales followed its cameo in Bong Joon-Ho's satirical comedy *Parasite*. (A five-hundred gram tin was spotted as part of the snack party eaten rebelliously by the interlopers in their wealthy employer's home.)

In an echo of the French winter trip that first inspired crisps in the UK, Bonilla crisps are distributed to British retailers thanks to the Spanish sailing holidays taken by a British tourist off the coast of Galicia. Clare Scott Dryden, whose family are keen sailors and moor their boat in a fishing village in A Coruña province, found herself chatting to the late César Bonilla, the founder's son, a 'great boatsman' who also tethered his motorboat in the same marina. 'He always used to bring crisps on the boat,' she told me. 'They were put into tins so they wouldn't stale in the salt air.' A la vista means ahoy! in Spanish sailing lingo: 'It's friendly in sailing terms, that's why the logo is a boat.'

'Don César', who won prizes in boyhood for his spearfishing and died aged ninety-one in early 2024, was a well-loved character whose first gig in the family business was to fry crisps alongside his mother and deliver them on his red Moto Guzzi motorbike. According to his obituary in *La Voz de Galicia*, in the 1980s he oversaw the opening and then later the running of the Bonilla factory in Sabón, which was churning out four hundred tonnes of crisps a year by the time he passed away.

Part of Bonilla's superiority lies in simplicity. The family uses local potatoes, the olive oil comes from southern Spain and they only season with sea salt – no additives. Although most potato chips have excess starch removed, Bonilla's extra-thin raw slices are washed especially thoroughly to remove as much of the starch as possible, so that the finished product is light and crispy. (Just Crisps in the UK also follows this method.) A person at the Bonilla factory hand-picks the largest crisps off the line for the tins, and the smaller ones go into bags.

When Clare struck a deal with the Bonilla family to distribute the crisps in the UK (as Bonilla Crisps) in 2010, British crisp eaters were instant admirers and the import business started to grow, with the blue sailboat logo appearing in food halls and farm shops and delis. Behind the scenes, as the order sheets lengthened, Clare began to learn about the peculiarities of transporting in excess of 200 pallets of crisps a year on trucks in tins and bags. Two stacked layers on top of each other – a full container of forty pallets – means the weight of the higher tins and bags can crush the crisps underneath, as she discovered. (When I spoke to her, she had just relinquished the Bonilla UK distribution rights to a large wholesaler. Whatever crisps she has left over, she said, she will keep eating happily.)

Bonilla commands a higher price point in the UK since it is a handmade product packaged for longevity. Nonetheless, the business was still growing year on year, selling in the trade to retailers such as Selfridges and Fortnum & Mason, both of which also enjoyed a 'bump' after *Parasite*, sending a sudden flurry of cases of crisp tins to Hong Kong and Korea. But the Covid-19 pandemic was the real boom time – 'our best year'. Forced to adapt, Clare brought some logistics away from the complex warehouse arrangements of normal trading and temporarily converted the yurt in her Hampshire garden into an additional storehouse rammed with crisp tins.

I think the light Bonilla style is what I have in mind in a corner bodega in Spain or France or Italy – that there will be a bag of wafery, extra-crispy crisps that don't try too hard to be anything else. This is not a low expectation. These are the same crisps that we ate on the campsite, and that followed on the Paris terraces in tiny white ramekins. They are crisps that have no pretences at all, except that they will not be the object of your attention.

If there is such a thing as the European crisp genre, there is also a genre of staggeringly geo-specific potato chips, most of which hail from Asia or America. Here in this category, in the music of strange crisp flavours, are the deep cuts: the sounds playing in the crisp-speakeasy underneath the aisle at the supermarket, the crisp equivalent of the basement jazz bar in Tokyo. I won't affix the brands at this point, but just imagine:

Pickled fish. Lemon tea. Cucumber. Doner kebab. Stewed beef noodles. Salted egg. Soft-shell crab. Coney Island mustard. Smoked Gouda. Hogg-tied. Hamburger seasoning. Honey butter. Roasted garlic oyster. Spicy crayfish. Finger-licking braised pork. Sesame sauce hotpot. Rose petal. Numb and spicy hotpot. Roasted fish. Blueberry.

This is a crisp banquet. And then add: grilled prawn with seafood sauce, a product of Lay's Thailand division that even without tasting or being able to procure, I am sure is equal to any prawn cocktail crisp.

I feel confident in this prejudice for one reason only: the audacity of the flavours that Lay's Asia seasoning team have produced. (The majority of the list above comes from Lay's and from American boutique brands.) This kind of pugnacious creativity is only achievable by popular mandate, so there must be a willing audience for the slavishly niche dish mimicry going on across the region's potato chips.

And Lay's is not the only brand in Asia working at this pitch. Calbee, a Japanese snack brand (which since 2018 has owned Seabrook in the UK, and also owns the Frito-Lay brand in Japan through an alliance with PepsiCo), has a massive commitment to variety in crisp form. Its 'cha chaan teng' series is inspired by old Hong Kong tearooms, with sweet and sour pork and satay beef noodle crisps. It even created a true novelty in 'wet' crisps, Nure Jaga (literally 'wet potato'), a semi-soggy texture that is apparently juicy to the bite and a delicacy to some.

Like Walkers and Golden Wonder, Calbee was a product of post-war entrepreneurialism, founded in 1949 as Matsuo Food Processing and rebranded in 1955 with a portmanteau of 'calcium' and 'vitamin B1'. Instant noodles were the growth product at first, but potato chips were added to huge success in the 1970s. Seaweed salt was its first flavoured crisp, introduced in 1976. Calbee invested heavily in its agronomic programme early on, and potatoes were treated with respect as a seasonal delicacy – a Hokkaido potato edition was available in autumn and winter, for example. And in the 1980s, *kataage* potato chips followed, which were kettle-cooked. Calbee experimented fearlessly: thicker and thicker cuts, and then thinner and thinner; skins on, skins off. Chocolate-tipped crisps were tried, as was a summer new-potato Natsu line. Compared with what was happening in UK crisp innovation in the 1970s and 1980s, the Japanese effort looks far more willing (or able) to take risks.

There is seemingly no flavour briefing so complex that it would daunt the flavour houses commissioned for Asian potato-chip manufacture. Jack 'n Jill, which is part of a Filipino brand, offers salmon sushi, black garlic tonkotsu ramen, green Sichuan peppercorn crisps and a Shake and Roll range that comes with a sachet of wasabi powder, a bit like the old Smith's salt sachet, to be shaken to taste.

But further than dancing imitatively around the wealth of flavour and *izakaya*-style pub snacking in Asian food, crisp manufacturers here have developed the precision to be regionally targeted. Calbee's seaweed salt punch, for example, is only available in the Tohoku, Kanto and Chubu regions of Japan. Its Hokkaido butter soy sauce crisps, similarly, are only available in Hokkaido, Tohoku and Chubu – the northern snow-country reaches of Japan, where the seafood catch is especially prized and delicious. *Shekwasha* flavour, or flat lemon, is only found on the southern island of Kyushu, a tribute to the *Citrus depressa* tree from which the very sour fruit is harvested in Okinawa, at the southern tip of the Japanese archipelago.

This is a different flex from the crisp market in the UK or even France, where cheese from Somerset or the Jura is a part of national sales, and where local taste becomes a selling point when its prestige is spread democratically through the medium of cheap potato chips.

But in Japan, at least, there is an inversion of this idea – local landscapes are reflected back into limited local crisp supply. Perhaps this explains in part why crisps aren't so fussed over in places such as Japan, a paradoxical effect of their brilliance being that no single flavour comes to represent an entire nation's tastes, as it does in the case of salt and vinegar in the UK, or cheese and onion in Ireland. Some flavours do break through – in the past five years honey butter crisps, for example, have become the crunch of choice in South Korea.

If there is localism in British crisps, it comes from expertise rather than flavour. The Walkers flagship factory in Leicester has multiple generations of the same family working on crisps, and longevity of service can run to thirty years. PepsiCo is one of the biggest employers in Leicester overall. It makes sense that a notion of a good crisp would all but get into the town water.

Among the more subtle territorial differences are the absences. In North Korea, snacking on commercially scaled and packaged products such as popped rice crisps has only recently entered popular culture, following a relaxation on production rules by the administration. Potato chips are available in limited quantities, and Supreme Leader Kim Jong Un sees the potato crop as a vital fallback in times of critical food shortages. Snacking at will, on products available at democratic scale, like a kind of universal snack suffrage, reflects a complacency about our political environment that we may never think twice about, regardless of the flavour.

Aside from Asia, America is the other superpower in regional potato-chip production. Fritos were a Texan product at their origin, and Lay's were from Atlanta; both were successful in their own right, but were changed by the corporate hyphenation that joined them together in 1961. Barely months after the business had launched, the success of Fritos meant that national distribution was weighed up as a possibility. In a 1934 issue of the *Brownsville Herald*, it was reported that the 'delicious Mexican crispie' sold in five-cent and picnic-sized glassine bags was already in demand from other cities and states, supplied by plants in Houston, Dallas and Tulsa. 'The officials of the company are now contemplating making Fritos a national product,' the report went on, 'and the first step toward this end will be the establishing of a new plant in another state.' This duly happened, and Fritos were no longer Texan but all-American.

Across the States, a number of much smaller potato-chip companies were thriving, in spite of Frito-Lay's now vast market coverage. Central, south-eastern and northern Ohio, for example, are the regions-within-a-region where Mikesell's potato chips do best. This is one of the oldest potato-chip companies anywhere – founded in 1910 by Daniel Mikesell from two rooms on South William Street in Dayton. Mikesell purchased some potato-chip equipment, started selling, and by the 1940s had added French-fried popcorn, crispettes and cheese wafers to his product range.

In south-west Iowa, meanwhile, Sterzing's is the best-selling potato chip. Founded, like Frito and Lay's, in the mid-1930s Great Depression, the company was an offshoot of Barney Sterzing's candy business. Sterzing chose to thin-slice and slow-fry the chips, which is how they're still made today, albeit sold in huge fourteen-ounce bags, redefining the meaning of family and sharing bags. (Two kilos would surely be enough for a rodeo.)

Another standout trait of American potato chips, or at least a rival trait to Asia, is that they can be expressive, to city-street level, of what urban centres mean for gourmet variation. Hal's of New York makes kosher dill pickle kettle chips, recalling the city's salt-brined vats of Kirby cucumbers. Chesapeake crab is the Southern flavour pride of Route 11 chips in Mount Jackson, Virginia: salty and spicy enough to mimic the fresh cooking of crab bushels in local restaurants.

I suppose the question comes back round to why we eat crisps in the first place. They could be substituted by something better – the real flavours they imitate. But crab is expensive. Great dill pickles are a hotly competitive foodstuff in New York. And flat lemon trees are rare. So the potato carries them for us, and a food odyssey is possible in minutes.

There's also the reality that these flavours are often playful reflections not of flavours but of complete meals – stewed beef, satay noodles, braised pork. Crisps are trifles next to the dishes that inspired them into being. In the official British citizenship test, questions on food culture reveal the enduringly limited horizons of complete meals that serve as national icons. In the arts and culture section of the Home Office questionnaire for British citizenship, a question asks: 'Which foods are linked to England?' To which fish and chips and roast beef are the 'correct' answers.

★

If Britain is a great crisp nation, why don't we have more regionally flavoured crisps? Part of the answer to this lies in competition. It is painfully, exorbitantly challenging to start a new crisp business from scratch. Those who manage it are joining a market where they may be locked out of good opportunities by the existing heritage muscle. If Britain ever considered itself to be an abundantly entrepreneurial crisp nation, it might now look in the mirror and see a distinct recession in its hairline.

Laura Bounds is the sole director of Kent Crisps, an artisan brand that takes its name from the coastal English county where it is based. Like others, it hand-cooks its crisps in batches, stirring the potato slices in oil to get a perfect crispness. But unlike a lot of the crisp pack, it goes out of its way to season the crisps with authentic local flavours: sea salt and vinegar with Biddenden cider, for example, or Ashmore cheese and onion. Both flavours use 'real' raw materials – cider from a nearby estate that grows Kentish apples, and a Cheddar-style farmhouse cheese made by Cheesemakers of Canterbury. 'Certain crisp companies might say they're using a certain beer. But it's matching, not incorporating the flavour,' she notes. 'How many chicken crisps are vegetarian?' (Almost all of them, with the possibly predictable exception of the Breton brand Les Brets' *poulet braisé*, which uses powdered roast chicken. Trust the French to take rotisserie seriously.)

Kent's most famous crisp flavour is oyster and vinegar, a clever play on salt inspired by the marine pickings at Whitstable Bay. Managing the business on her own with six people on the payroll, Laura as the female owner of a handcooked crisp company without a male business partner is a rarity in the UK. 'The sector is extremely intimidating,' she said, her newborn baby asleep in her arms. 'It's a dog-eat-dog world in crisps. Some very big companies who have market share are bullish. It's been a fight over the last ten years.'

The crisp business is very male. 'So, so male dominated,' Laura says. 'I've been fighting the market leaders my entire career. We're now finding it amusing when we're negotiating. But being a young female business owner, it used to be challenging.'

Little surprise that so many independents have fallen away in the last ten years.

There are lots of dangers to dodge. Cashflow is one of the bluntest problems that crisp beginners encounter, particularly when trying to weigh up the benefit of bulk-ordering things like oil, packaging and seasoning. And it 'costs a lot to start and fund a crisp business', for one thing, Laura says, given all the specialist equipment that you 'can't just knock up in a garden shed', despite what the typical kitchen-table origin stories lead us to believe. She contrasts crisp-industry market entry to the relative ease of joining the condiments sector, which has plenty of indies, thanks to the low start-up costs. Anyone can make jam at their kitchen table, but not everyone can fork out for high-spec crisp fryers.

'A lot have fallen short by thinking they can make a multi-million-pound business. There is a lack of knowledge of how tough it is to make profit in this sector.' As a result, 'People have sold out to bigger brands, and there has been a lot of consolidation.'

But what's happened in the wake of consolidation, she adds, is that 'there isn't clarity [about sourcing and production]. We use [quality-assured] Red Tractor potatoes: they're all British.'

Kent Crisps now turns over just under £1.5 million a year, and has seen good year-on-year growth since 2017. But it was founded, back in 2011, almost as a side hustle by an estate tourism business that already owned some farmland. 'They came up with the concept,' Laura explained. 'I knew its potential.'

She joined the business a couple of years after it started, and a few years after that she was overseeing the running of the whole show. In 2017 she organised a self-funded management buyout of the business, aware that the shareholder was hoping to move towards an exit. 'I had come on board relatively young, with quite a clear vision for the business. I knew what it could do.'

The business had been built around the principle of provenance. 'It was the first hand-cooked crisp producer that said, let's take local ingredients, what our county has to offer in amazing food production, that cheese and that cider, and let's take the county as a destination in terms of tourism.'

Just as restaurant-goers will be accustomed to seeing the provenance of produce listed on the menu nowadays, so most crisp companies have caught up with the trend. But back in 2011, the idea seemed like madness to many in the industry. 'Why would anyone add to their cost of goods?' the thinking went. 'You'd reduce your margin.' It of course costs more to buy farmhouse cheese, to pay for 'kilos and kilos' of the stuff, and then pay the seasoning labs to powder the cheese down and take out the water. And that's before the issue of intellectual property comes into play, since a good flavouring idea is by no means protected.

> I've had our flavours copied. It's heart-breaking when someone takes your whole idea. The flavour houses do have a set agreement in place that the seasoning they agree to your spec is solely for you. But for my lamb and rosemary flavour, someone matched the flavour. You don't have to use the same ingredients to get the same outcome.

Although there are agreements in place, with food it's very difficult to claim sole ownership over a combination of natural flavours. 'You can sign NDAs and ask people not to rip off this recipe. But you can match things so closely with other spices.'

A missing edge, Laura felt, was the design of the packaging. It should make greater play of the Kentish landscapes, she felt, with commissioned photography rather than stock images. She has since heard tales of American and Chinese air passengers visiting Leeds Castle after eating her crisps on the plane. 'For us, our main uniqueness is we're flying the British flag and representing our county. For us that's how we're driving export as a growth part of our business. In the UK market there is volume to be had out there, but it's not the same.'

And here, in the negotiating fray for big contracts with airlines, travel companies, foreign retailers and food service, is where good but onerous money can be made. 'Some of those contracts in a tough year were amazing,' Laura Bounds told me. 'Equally, you lose them as well. I would prefer to have multiple wholesalers who are doing £50k a year than a million-pound contract.'

She gives an example of a deal in which she was trying to be listed on a cruise line and a major brand joined the bidding by going in at below cost price. They were loss-leading to gain market share, simply because they could afford to. 'It's all very commercialised, flexing muscle and volume. Doing a deal and undercutting. That's a huge part of our sector.' But, she adds, 'I've always run in my lane.'

This is where staying small can be a strength, in the ratio of turnover to profit. Other companies in the premium independent range might turn over more, Laura said, but 'I would rather have a sustainable business even if it means sometimes turning over less.' The reality is that where America has good coverage of independent crisp brands playing up to their individual states' flavours, the UK has only a handful.

If there were no limit in the crisp lab, I would hazard a try for some combinations I love. Buttermilk soda bread and honey. Loch Fyne langoustines and lemon. Pear and Stilton. And perhaps from city to city there would be crisp variations, not just preferences. Lorne sausage in Glasgow. Pie and mash in London. Strawberry-fool crisps in the summer, roast chestnut crisps in winter.

10

fieldwork

ou can't get lost,' someone promised me ominously last summer, outlining a hike in Perthshire. I did get lost, and my rescue route cut straight across the unthinkable: a giant potato field. Nettled grass and a tangled riverbank beckoned in the other direction, lunchtime sun getting fiercer. Knowing that I must be breaking at least three written and unwritten rules of the countryside, I decided to give crop trespassing a go.

Solanum tuberosum is not nice to walk through. The soil, built up like molehills, crumbled underfoot. These ridges are farmer-made, shaped to prevent the tubers from getting sunburnt at their shallow growing depth. With my dog following behind me, the crop shivered noisily as we made our progress. It was slower and tougher than I expected it to be. The spuds grow like rubble in the earth, and above ground the plants follow the sun bushily upwards before offering white and purple fingernail-shaped petals shortly before the tubers mature. I struggled on, then stopped: potato leaves are ticklish and tall enough to feel as if you are wading in a river of weeds. Somewhere, too, I imagined I could sense the steel of a farmer's disapproval sighted on me (and on the dog). I turned back round to face the nettles.

Tim Rooke is a man who has spent a lifetime – some of it forbearing – in the sensory world of potato fields. He is the fourth generation of his family to farm on the eastern slopes of the Pennines in England, mainly dealing in a rotation of potatoes and wheat across a thousand acres of land. 'Certainly good potato land,' Tim says, 'but it's stony and undulating.'

Raw potatoes can go in different industrial directions – towards crisps, chips, snacks, fresh bags, ready meals, dog food – and each direction requires a different type of tuber. The trends up to 2020 showed a very slight incline in crisping potatoes, but largely crisps are a flat line. In any case, Tim doesn't see his work by category. 'We're not potato farmers,' he said firmly. 'We're farmers who grow potatoes.'

The Rookes started with two hundred acres, and widened their holdings through a mixture of ambition, bank loans and the boom in the British crisp business that took hold in the 1970s. I spoke to Tim on the phone for hours as he went about his work: he took calls in the field, pulling up irrigators; in the yard, waiting to confer with workers; and once or twice through booming speaker phones on the road to the airport or the races. He was very rarely at home.

'I've missed that many things in my life because of potatoes,' he told me. 'Friends ringing up saying shall we do this or that. You need to be dedicated. I remember watching my father struggling in a field in October and thinking, "There's more to life than this."'

When Tim left school in 1974, with five O levels, he didn't want to go further into education. 'I just wanted to come home,' he said, but he wasn't especially keen on joining the farm trade, either: 'I didn't want to disappoint my father.' His father had a 'low-paying' contract at the time with Cadbury's for its instant potato mash product, Smash, made from dehydrated spud powder. A television advert for this just-add-water idea made fun of how British people boiled potatoes laboriously to make ordinary

mash, and their chosen device to make this point was to depict a
board meeting of aliens discussing the inadequacy of life on Earth.

ALIEN 1: On your last trip, did you discover what the Earth
People eat?

ALIEN 2: They eat a great many of *these* [assistant alien holds
up a potato]. They peel them with their metal knives. Boil
for twenty of their minutes. Then they smash them all to bits!
[General hilarity.]

This kind of product was less amusing for the farmers. 'You
couldn't progress your business; there were only so many potatoes you could bag. We ditched Cadbury's, and started getting
reasonable money from United Biscuits.'

In 1973, the year before Tim left school, United Biscuits-owned
KP Snacks launched the first packets of Hula Hoops potato rings,
with McCoy's premium crisps following soon in the KP brand
portfolio. Kenyon Produce had been making pickles and jams in
Rotherham since the mid-nineteenth century, passing between
different owners until it got a lead on the peanut butter market in
the 1950s and attracted the interest of snack maker United Biscuits
in 1968. UB was then itself acquired by Germany's Intersnack in
2013, which in turn bought up Tyrrells and Popchips in 2018, cornering a good share of the UK snacking market.

As British families began to sample the delights of Hula Hoops,
the food-manufacturing industry had begun its awakening into
an era where plain food could be dismissed as primitive (boiled

potatoes), and convenience food lauded as intelligent (dehydrated potatoes). Crisps, which were fried rather than dried potatoes, fell somewhere between these categories, neither a humdrum basic nor a game-changing reinvention, more of an entertaining, exotic intermission between the two. Hula Hoops were considered crisps, but made from dehydrated potato flakes.

Once at the helm of the business, Tim decided to move operations into the now 'cut-throat' world of crisping potatoes: cut-throat not only because of the market, but also because of risk. For the receiving crispers, competition was bitterly alive. Even today, a dominant Walkers alone relies on six or seven dozen supplier farms in the UK, and there are also KP, Tayto Group, Seabrook and other smaller crisp factories to supply around the country, some of which also make crisps for private labels.

Farmers, however, are not so much in tension with each other for business contracts, as with the manufacturers and the potato merchants who pass on the terms and prices. It's an unforgiving trade: the crisping industry is very specific on what it does or doesn't accept. 'My opinion is that the attention to detail is tighter than for a chipping potato or fresh,' Tim said. 'The criteria for success are tighter.'

A large crisp manufacturer does not usually speak directly to the farm, but delegates the contracts to intermediary potato merchants, such as Cockerill, who deliver the contractors' seed potatoes and send other subcontractors to collect the potatoes at different seasonal points of the year. This could be early on in the growing year, known as lifting potatoes 'green top', if the variety is suitable; but more commonly it happens after autumn harvest or later in winter from cold stores on the farm.

Supplier farms all face the same workload and worry: pulling up irrigators in the field; anxious and constant phone-checking for the weather; fiddly temperature controlling of winter barn-fuls of potatoes (a stored crop can be 'shocked' and ruined by a sudden mercury drop); digging of soil samples sent off to the Department for Environment, Food and Rural Affairs to check for free-living eelworm; Christmases waiting for next year's prices to be set by the crisp makers (usually PepsiCo goes first); fixing of potato washers; buying of half-a-million-pound harvesters; more repairing of potato washers; and just endless struggling to find labourers, post-Brexit, who will do the hot, cold and thankless jobs that are essential to the business of crisps.

Some of the variables are deep-set by geological time. You can't change the lie of a particular patch of British land without the workings of thousands of years. Parts of Norfolk have the fin-est, flattest potato acres in the country, with its spuds destined mostly for fresh supermarket bags, while Scotland is the leader in growing seed potatoes because of its cool climate, which helps to deter virus-carrying aphids. These kinds of advantages may fol-low ancient roots, but there are little cracks starting to appear in the map of who farms which potatoes where.

'The problem we have is, it's risk against return,' Tim said. 'A crop of potatoes was £1,000 per acre [to grow] twenty years ago, now it's £2,000 plus. If things go wrong after a drought, we lose more money. There are some potatoes that give up on the first sign of hot weather,' he added, referring to the recent, deleterious effects of the 2022 heatwave in Britain.

During that summer in the UK, potato farmers warned that yields would drop in volume and quality because of the drought. Half of the potato crop in England failed. The costs of fertiliser, electricity and fuel also spiked – quadrupling in the case of fuel – at the same time as the fields were baking, creating a nasty cash-flow tourniquet. Some costs might ease off, but temperatures will continue on this punishing trajectory unless climate action intensifies. There used to be three years in every ten that would require heavy irrigation, Tim says, but now that ratio looks uncertain, even wishful, and the more water-pumping required, the higher the costs.

At farm level, this is worrying. The £1,000-per-acre benchmark to grow crisping potatoes twenty years ago would include 'rent [if a field is rented from another farmer while their own land is on rotation], the seed, the fertiliser, labour, fuel, electricity, everything', Tim says. 'Now it's over £2,000 an acre, and our margin hasn't altered a lot, but failure is high risk. If you're growing six or seven hundred acres, that's £1.5 million invested in crisp fields, and it all depends on the weather. Things have altered. Global warming is increasing. Failure is more expensive than what it used to be.'

Like the American writer David Foster Wallace once said of the lobster, there is probably more to know about potato farming than you might in fact care to know. Some things stand out, however.

That farmers consider a mature potato crop to be 'dead' reversed my vocabulary of how 'fresh' food might be described in practice. Unless they are an 'early' variety, potatoes need to be dead before they are harvested, to allow for the sugar in the tubers to be excreted through the foliage. The sweeter a tuber, the darker it fries, and so lifting the potatoes at exactly the right moment – and avoiding the hazards of frost and excess wetness in the field – is critical to the colour of what the end consumer eats. 'If it never dies, it would never fry,' is Tim's motto on the matter.

And then there's farmyard equipment. It perhaps shouldn't be a big surprise, given the cost of even a mid-market dishwasher, but the price tags took me aback: £200,000 for a new specialist potato washer, for example, puts the scale of the supplier's gamble in perspective. There are rewards, however, if things go right.

It can be hard to judge how well off farmers are, given that they usually keep at least three grades of vehicle on their land – a hopeless banger, a dusty pick-up truck and possibly a nice car hiding in a garage somewhere. Which of these best represents their fortune is not always clear. A crisping farmer with a similar acreage as Tim, however, might expect £100,000 in profit in an OK year, and £300,000–£400,000 in a good year when the weather and yields and quality have gone to plan.

That might sound to many people like insurance enough against the risk of crop wipeouts. But in the background are ever-lengthening shadows of the way in which we take agriculture for granted, and of our complacency that everything we enjoy in the post-industrial age is replenishable.

This is why there is a possible tipping point in view, where British potato-crisp makers might need British potato farmers more than British potato farmers need British potato-crisp makers. The business of water and weather is integral to this tipping point. Potatoes are 80 per cent water, and the soil in which they grow must be irrigated to very precise levels. Unless local precipitation is sufficient, 'rain tractors' or umbrella sprinklers can pump out around twelve thousand gallons of water an hour, a way of substituting rainfall that makes bigger potato fields hiss with the sound of water.

But that volume of water cannot come off the mains supply, so it is pumped from rivers, reservoirs or boreholes. All these options are tightly controlled by the Environment Agency. If there is a drought – and there will be droughts – the farmer's options shrivel. 'There's a lot that is out of our hands,' Tim said. 'Some of the quality is achievable more by good weather than good farming.'

Furrows and fields, even the humble tractor, often find themselves on crisp packets as classical emblems of farming that make crisps happen. I've now started to think about the rivers and reservoirs absent in the picture.

When Tim Rooke sees a packet of crisps in a shop, the first thing he does is look at the back to check the best before date. Now, I do the same.

The freshness of most of the crisps on UK shop shelves is an aspect of their vulnerability and desirability that I had taken for granted. Stale crisps like the ones schoolchildren ate at the Saturday matinee cinema in the 1950s are rare, and a packet of limp, even damp crisps is usually the result of a tiny, heart-breaking hole in the plastic bag. But as a reborn crisp consumer I have tried to scrutinise the distance between today's date and the best before date, and guess how fresh the potatoes were, depending on the time of year.

Although many crispers package their wares using high-spec machinery and thick film flushed with nitrogen that can prolong shelf life for up to six months, the point of crisps is that they are a fast-moving inventory. Crispers are increasingly using data analysis to perfect this timing, understanding the right moment at which to draw on each store.

Crucially, potatoes keep well if the harvest is good quality and stored correctly. This was true even when early storage was primitively built, and the spuds were chucked into pits covered with lime, or clamped in straw bales. Healthy potatoes harvested carefully to avoid bruising (that little brown spot you sometimes see at the corner of a crisp is a bruise) and kept at the correct temperature can last the winter – a provision that often made the difference between life and death.

Tim also scrutinises the packet code that tells you the variety (not always shown) and the location of production (also not always shown in detail, although Kettle Brand in America has an impressive potato-tracking feature on its website, allowing you to see the supplier farm closest to your zip code). He doesn't touch Pringles, which are made outside the UK. 'I also look at the size of the crisp and the shape, to see if it's longer and oval,' he mentioned. 'Proper crisping potatoes are round.'

For all the vastness of parents and progeny in the potato family, wild and cultivated, only a few of its members are suitable for the job, for reasons of safety as much as the potatoes' varying fry properties. Chris Dimelow, the head of the European potato and tortilla platform for Walkers, told me that the 'potato flavour is so important. We do want to celebrate that the crisp is a potato.' It may sound obvious, but it is in fact 'complicated', he added. 'Because it's not just any potato. My team is making sure the crisp itself is at standard. [First we make a] great crisp that then has a great flavour.'

How does he define a great crisp? 'We have an intuition, we know what a good crisp is,' comes the not unreasonable answer. And the notion is taken seriously. Chris, at one point, even compares production to protecting precious antiques. 'We try to turn the bed of crisps in the most gentle way,' he says, 'to protect the crisps like a Ming vase.'

Analytical tools follow the crisps second by second along their brief linear progress: potato to packet takes just three or four minutes. Though any modern factory might not look too crowded with humans, there are technical experts on hand for each how-to: how to peel a potato, how to slice a potato, how to fry a potato, how long to fry it for, ridge shape or flat, how to bag the end product. The temperature of the cooking oil can be dialled up and down subtly, as much as subtlety is afforded at industrial scale. Each of these aspects involves software and expensive machinery, but a human 'quality wall' does pick the product off the line periodically and sample it against a reference, to check for quality. 'They are able to say, "No, that's not good enough,"' Chris says.

The narrowness of the field of crisping potatoes is an old problem. Ever since crisps began to be made in England at factory scale in the 1920s, manufacturers have known that only a handful of potato varieties work well in the fryer. Much more recently, a danger was also uncovered when potatoes are fried at high temperatures.

If the cooking temperature exceeds 120°C, it can trigger the formation of the chemical compound acrylamide. The presence of acrylamide in starchy foods was discovered by Swedish scientists in 2002, and food regulations swiftly introduced since then have prevented it from surfacing into a public anxiety. But if left to accumulate in uncontrolled levels, acrylamide reputedly has potential to be harmful through long-term exposure. It can be carcinogenic to humans, and may affect neurological and reproductive health, too, according to a paper published in the *Journal of Experimental Botany*.

Companies now invest huge amounts in potato varieties or lower-temperature cooking methods that reduce this risk. The collection of measures now in place across food regulation bodies also focuses on potato storage at not-too-cool temperatures (to avoid the formation of acrylamide-forming sugars) and carefully monitoring the fry colour of the product. Acrylamide levels in crisps have fallen considerably in the past twenty years as a result of this strict quality control.

Given that I started eating crisps as a child in the 1980s, I had at least a decade of voluminously consuming a product that was not as harmless as it seemed at the time. I often used to throw the tomato sandwiches from my packed lunches into the bin at school, annoyed by the way the seeds and juices seeped into the pappy bread until the sandwich was a soggy, cling-filmed pulp. It made me seek the crunch of a crisp packet all the more determinedly, but I was unwittingly isolating a low-lying hazard as my only source of lunchtime nutrition.

I began to credit how little thought I had given to the impression that a part of my childhood could seemingly be picked off the shelf in a supermarket, any day I pleased, almost in perpetuity. This impression was not completely real. The industrial recipe has changed, the potato varieties have advanced, the crisp flesh is a different colour, the sunflower oil is less fatty, and it turns out the carcinogenic properties are now seemingly negligible. (Whether it would really stop me if they weren't is a question I am unable to answer properly.) And this began to nudge me towards another question. The difference between crisps then and now is incontrovertible, so why was I so convinced that I remembered what 1989 ready salted actually tasted like?

I stopped eating tomato sandwiches as soon as I had the chance, but the miserable, unsalted experience of eating them is close at hand. I can still taste something I disliked and have not tasted for thirty years. Evidently I carried on with crisps. But do

I actually possess distinct memories of their former taste? Is it the memory that has an attachment to a factual detail of flavour, bookmarked by the crisps, rather than crisps creating a memory of a flavour itself?

In talking to people about the topic of this book as I wrote it, I heard many perfectly preserved crisp capsules. A friend's mother would eat salt and vinegar crisps with her in bed as a treat when she had been poorly. Someone else recounted how they escaped their unhappy family on Saturday mornings by hiding with newspapers and crisps in the attic. Another told me how they stood perusing crisps in a Honduran bodega next to two customers doing the same, but carrying AK-47s over their shoulders like tote bags.

My own crisp memories have almost nothing in common with each other, such is the size of the library of references. I remember the special strangeness at gingerly organised events in the aftermath of the first Covid-19 lockdown, where almost everyone covered 'catering' by providing a bowl not of loose crisps but of crisp packets – one socially sealed pouch per guest, to be eaten awkwardly through lifted masks. I remember opening presents with my family on Christmas morning with crisps and wine, both doubly good for being before their usual watersheds. I remember coming back from London to Glasgow on the five-hour train with my dog, having underestimated how much food to bring for him, and realising that after he had eaten my ham sandwich, he was now looking at my crisps. He ate them without question, though I felt guilty. I also remember tea and crisps with friends on the summit of Ben More on Mull, the first Munro I climbed. I remember hating London park picnics but always believing that a big bag of crisps would itself be a friend to all the other weird snack bits and pieces gathered, and if not, crisps would suffice on their own. A food that does not discriminate between emergency, achievement and celebration has to be worthy of its place in all scenarios.

Of course, it's not just crisps that unlock and attach to memory among things we eat. But when I tried to interrogate my memory for other commonplace and beloved things in my diet, such as toast or coffee or pasta, I found it harder to locate quite as many specific or isolated scenes.

Crisps had kept hold of moments from the past that I would not know to look for by the things they contained alone. Whatever the truth about our olfactory processing of memory, these crisp-eating scenes seemed to come from a neurological shelter that was not damaged or obscured by the time from distant to recent experience, saving something from memory blindness.

Old packets of crisps periodically wash up on beaches intact, and are reported in newspapers as if shipwrecked pieces of treasure had drifted ashore. The last one was a 1960s packet of ready salted that turned up in Norfolk. A 1970s packet washed on to Devon's Saunton Sands beach a few years before.

When a crisp packet bobs through the water sixty years from now and blows into the dunes somewhere, bleached by sea salt and age, it will be a plastic feather of time. Just as you look at a feather, and wonder about the bird, the stranded crisp packet will bring questions. Where did this come from? Who ate the contents? And just perhaps, on the eve of a new century, why don't they make this flavour any more?

epilogue: chip lover's hotline

I made a crisp sandwich for breakfast. Streaky bacon, toasted white bloomer, Cheddar cheese, wisps of salad, a bit of butter and a packet of Walkers Marmite crisps (now tragically discontinued) in between the slices. Smashed, not squashed.

I had made a note to eat crisps for breakfast when I found out this was commonplace in the early crisp days of the 1920s, half-expecting the experience to give me a costumed feeling for life in the inter-war years, when crisps on a breakfast plate of bacon and egg would not have turned heads. Crisps at 10 a.m. on the weekend felt a little decadent, but they blended in so well with the sandwich that I forgot about the promise of time travel.

Yet there is something in the universality of crisps' appeal that does vivify the strangers who've eaten them in the past and the present. Though he wrote about potato chips, rather than potato crisps, the Chilean poet Pablo Neruda captured this perfectly in his poem 'Ode to French Fries', in which (more poetically) he writes a love letter to how boiling things in oil is a delight so irresistible it works anywhere, touching something eternal. This statement can hardly be denied – and it's an incontrovertible truth that speaks to a short bracket of time in which the industrial world became the global palate.

I ate my crisp breakfast sandwich on Sunday 17 December, and the best before date, as I turned over the packet, was stamped as

16 March the following year. Just as Walkers claimed, 16 March would be a Saturday. Everything underpinning my love of crisps seemed to run like clockwork.

I'm still complacent, and I am not a reformed crisp character. I have little desire to be. A bag of root vegetable crisps that forsakes the flavoured potato and presents instead parsnips, sweet potato and wrinkled beetroot is not enough. The realm of crisps is fuller and more detailed in my mind's eye, but its sensory value is unchanged.

I decided it was time to tidy up the empty packets. To clear crisps from view. My home was scattered with a colourful surface litter of empty crisp packets, and I couldn't deny the odd feelings they provoke. My desk was stacked high with them, an in-tray of crinkled plastic. I had finished looking at them, and they had become popular with my open summer windows' draught of flies and wasps. Now, in wintertime, I'd heard the first suspicious scurrying of mice.

There, as I folded up the packets, on the back of a packet of Kettle Chips I spied a phone number, an 0800 number for the company's 'Chip Lover's Hotline'.

This phone line, I could tell from its silly wink-wink name, would not have any answers. But I called it. I heard the ten digits beep through, and realised that this was a call to the unknown. What would anyone phone this number for? What was there to ask? I waited for it to connect. And then, in the sound of a pre-recorded voice, were the 'press 1 for, press 2 for, press 3 for' options for speaking to the purchasing, warehousing and admin departments of Kettle Chips.

epilogue

And a final option, 'other queries'. I pressed the button.

Straight to a nameless Vodafone voicemail: leave a message after the tone.

I didn't hang up. But what could I say? I thought of saying the only thing I know is really true about this subject. I put the phone down. And I said the message to myself.

I have eaten so many crisps.

acknowledgements

Thank you: Robbie Guillory for stopping to hear out the idea for this book on a Glasgow street corner; all the team at Faber, especially Fiona Crosby for her insight and support; and loving thanks to my father for his kindest encouragement. Thanks to the brilliant Paul Reich for taking my photograph, and to Miranda York for publishing my first crisp essay in the food journal *Toast*. Finest crisps also for their solidarity during the writing period: Clothilde Redfern, Matt Fountain, Jennie Middlemiss, Malcolm Campbell, Sarah Bernstein, Andrew Meehan, Alex McCartney-Moore, Christiano Mere and the Glad Writers. And to the interviewees who shared their time and stories of the crisp world, thank you most of all.

notes

Prologue

Old English crisp, *for curly*: Oxford English Dictionary, https://www.oed.
  com/dictionary/crisp_adj?tab=meaning_and_use# 7814573.
Lay's available almost everywhere: PepsiCo Careers website, pepsicojobs.com.
egg flavour is derived from a 'natural aroma': information provided by
  Patatas Torres via email, February 2023.
On the streets of Madrid: Inma Garrido, 'Las fábricas de patatas fritas y
  aperitivos que alegran Madrid', *El Pais*, 13 March 2021
social part of eating: Michel Onfray, *Appetites for Thought: Philosophers and
  Food*, trans. Donald Barry and Stephen Muecke (London: Reaktion, 2015),
  p. 38.
reduced chocolate rations handed to surveilled citizens: George Orwell,
  Nineteen Eighty-Four (1949; London: Penguin Twentieth-Century
  Classics, 1989), p. 28.
the link between auditory cues and perception of quality and crispness: Z. M.
  Vickers, 'Sensory, Acoustical, and Force-Deformation Measurements of
  Potato Chip Crispness', *Journal of Food Science*, 52 (1987): 138–40;
  M. Zampini and C. Spence, 'The Role of Auditory Cues in Modulating
  the Perceived Crispness and Staleness of Potato Chips', *Journal of Sensory
  Studies*, 19 (2004): 347–63.
*Paiges . . . wound up . . . Lennard's Crisps Limited, dissolved 1932. Krunch
  Potato Crisps Limited, dissolved in 1948*: National Archives Public
  Records, Board of Trade, accessed online.
you become a New Yorker: Colson Whitehead, *The Colossus of New York*
  (2003; London: Little, Brown, 2018).
J. R. Cullip . . . wrote a definitive-sounding rebuttal: 'Letter to the Editor: Take a
  Pinch of Dry Salt', *Financial Times*, 28 May 1985, p. 17.

ex-Walkers chief executive Martin Glenn's 'video book': Martin Glenn, *The Best Job in the World* (London: Compton House Publishing, 2005).

The court ruled that Pringles satisfied two tests: Revenue & Customs *v* Procter & Gamble UK [2009] EWCA Civ 407.

global crown of snacking: Per-capita volume sales in the snack food market worldwide by country in 2022, Statista.com, accessed February 2024.

$98 billion market: Potato chips – worldwide, Statista.com, accessed February 2024.

prompted by a faulty IT upgrade: Finvola Dunphy, 'Walkers Confirms Cause of Crisps Shortage as Snack Fans Express Their Displeasure', *Leicestershire Live*, 9 November 2021.

Loving crisps is one of the most abundant things the British do economically: 'UK Crisps, Savoury Snacks and Nuts Market Report', 2023, Mintel.

props in more serious drama: various cases, the National Archives.

1. Very Plain

stagecoach route that once paused at coaching inns: Brenda J. Buchanan, 'The Great Bath Road, 1700–1830', *Bath History* IV (Bath: Millstream Books, 1992), p. 80.

one of the biggest crisp factories in the world: Pepsico.co.uk, 'We're Investing £58 Million in Walkers Manufacturing Site in Leicester'.

Walkers swears is always a Saturday: Quality control FAQ at walkers.co.uk.

the roughly 186,000 tonnes of crisps sold annually in the UK: Potato chips manufacture sales volume UK 2008–2022, Statista.com, accessed February 2024.

'crisp scare' that made Central Television news: Central News East, 19 July 1989. Media Archive for Central England.

toxins that would require heavy soil treatment: 'EFRI ELiS: Bioweathering Dynamics and Ecophysiology of Microbially Catalyzed Soil Genesis of Martian Regolith', NASA website.

Golden Wonder, which Brown exhibited at the Smithfield Show in London:

notes

'Rearer of the "Golden Wonder" Potato: Testimonial Presented to
Mr John Brown, Arbroath', *Scotsman*, 10 February 1936, p. 15; 'Man
Who Introduced the Golden Wonder: Late Mr John Brown, Peasiehill,
Arbroath', *Scotsman*, 18 April 1938, p. 16.

moved on to 'better' crisping varieties: email from Tayto Group
representative, February 2024.

Everybody Eats 'Um, Everybody Likes 'Um: *Toledo Union Journal*, 28 April
1950.

FL 2027 patented potato: National Center for Biotechnology Information,
'PubChem Patent Summary for US-6940004-B2, Potato cultivar FL 2027',
https://pubchem.ncbi.nlm.nih.gov/patent/US-6940004-B2.

potatoes don't appreciate long-haul journeys: T. M. Robertson et al., 'Starchy
Carbohydrates in a Healthy Diet: The Role of the Humble Potato',
Nutrients, 10 (2018): 1764.

Soil that harbours free-living eelworms, for example: 'Free-Living Nematodes
and Their Impact on the Yield and Quality of Field Crops', Agriculture
and Horticulture Development Board, online at AHDB website.

Almost all potatoes emanated from the fecundity of Latin America: Hugo
Campos and Oscar Ortiz (eds), *The Potato Crop: Its Agricultural,
Nutritional and Social Contribution to Humankind* (Cham: Springer,
2020).

governor of the Bahamas sent a gift box of potatoes to Virginia in the 1620s:
Linhai Zhang et al., 'Inferred Origin of Several Native American Potatoes
from the Pacific Northwest and Southeast Alaska Using SSR Markers',
Euphytica, 174 (2010): 15–29.

food-loving French novelist Alexandre Dumas père: Alexandre Dumas,
From Absinthe to Zest: An Alphabet for Food Lovers, trans. Alan and Jane
Davidson (1978; repr. London: Penguin, 2011).

Andean potatoes burst into growth: 'Andean Potato (*S. tuberosum* subsp.
andigenum)', Cultivariable.com.

Peru's Tiyapuy: 'Productos de papas nativas peruanas', tiyapuy.com.

Nikolai Vavilov, a dashing, principled botanist: Igor G. Loskutov, *Vavilov and His Institute: A History of the World Collection of Plant Genetic Resources in Russia* (Rome: International Plant Genetic Resources Institute, 1999); 'Wartime Activities of the Vavilov Institute', *Proceedings on Applied Botany Genetics and Breeding*, 182 (2021): 151–62.

Charles III, who sent botanists Hipólito Ruiz and José Pavón: Daniela Bleichmar, 'A Botanical Reconquista', in *Visible Empire: Botanical Expeditions and Visual Culture in the Hispanic Enlightenment* (Chicago: University of Chicago Press, 2012).

Darwin had brought back: Jean Beagle Ristaino and Donald H. Pfister, '"What a Painfully Interesting Subject": Charles Darwin's Studies of Potato Late Blight', *BioScience*, 66 (2016): 1035–45.

Department of Agriculture professors travelled to Russia: Loskutov, *Vavilov and His Institute*.

he had gathered Solanum tuberosum *growing in the crevices*: letter from John Maclean to Sir William Jackson Hooker, from Lima, 12 May 1849, Kew Royal Botanic Gardens Archive.

Recent analysis by the Natural History Museum in London and the Max Planck Institute in Germany: R. M. Gutaker et al., 'The Origins and Adaptation of European Potatoes Reconstructed from Historical Genomes', *Nature Ecology & Evolution*, 3 (2019): 1093–101.

The food historian Rebecca Earle has argued: R. Earle, *Feeding the People: The Politics of the Potato* (Cambridge: Cambridge University Press, 2020).

Dumas describes as 'absurd prejudices': Dumas, *From Absinthe to Zest*.

citations for the potato: Jack Lynch (ed.), *Samuel Johnson's Dictionary: Selections from the 1755 Work that Defined the English Language* (London: Atlantic, 2004).

Danish pastor Lauritz Minis from the island of Funen: 'Kartoflens historie', Danish Potato Museum website.

famines were becoming commonplace: G. Alfani and C. Ó. Gráda, 'Famines in Europe: An Overview', in Alfani and Ó Gráda (eds), *Famines in European History* (Cambridge: Cambridge University Press, 2017), pp. 1–24.

potato found a cheerleader: biography of Antoine Augustin Parmentier,

notes

Palace of Versailles website.

a section of the Jardins des Tuileries: Dumas, *From Absinthe to Zest*.

American slave narratives feature potatoes: Federal Writers' Project, *Slave Narratives*, esp. vol. 12: Ohio (1936). https://www.loc.gov/items/mesn120.

visiting the cottage of the Groot family in Nuenen: Brigit Katz, 'The Untold Story of Van Gogh's Once-Maligned Masterpiece, "The Potato Eaters"', *Smithsonian* magazine, 7 October 2021; '6 Things You Need to Know about Van Gogh's Potato Eaters', Van Gogh Museum website.

potato farming should be encouraged again: Pratik Jakhar, 'North Korea: Potato Propaganda Is Back . . . But What Does It Mean?', BBC Monitoring, 19 December 2020.

kept the potatoes from deadly frosts: Loskutov, *Vavilov and His Institute*.

recipe for a crisp omelette starter: Ferran Adrià, *The Family Meal* (London: Phaidon, 2011).

chuño in Latin America: Alejandra Osorio, 'Why Chuño Matters: Rethinking the History of Technology in Latin America', *Technology and Culture*, 63 (2022): 808–29.

four and a half pounds of potatoes: Sarah O'Connor, 'Researching the Irish Famine', National Library of Ireland website.

twelve hundred champagne bottles: National Records of Scotland, Edinburgh.

The Cook's Oracle: William Kitchiner, *The Cook's Oracle; and Housekeeper's Manual* (1817); accessed via Project Gutenberg.

interesting concoction for purple-fleshed vitelotte *potatoes*: M.-A. Carême, *Le cuisinier parisien* (1828).

cookery writer Urbain Dubois: Urbain Dubois, *Nouvelle cuisine bourgeoise pour la ville et pour la campagne* (10th edition, Paris, 1890).

setting was the restaurant at Moon's Lake House: 'Moon's Lake House, Saratoga Lake', Saratoga Springs Public Library, New York Heritage Digital Collections.

George Crum: 'George Crum and the Potato Chip', Saratoga County History Center via Brookside Museum website.

Good accident: photograph of manuscript, George S. Bolster Collection.

restaurant manager, Hiram S. Thomas: portrait of head waiter and restaurant
manager Hiram S. Thomas (1890), Schomburg Center for Research
in Black Culture, Photographs and Prints Division, New York Public
Library; Suzanne Spellen, 'The Hiram S. Thomas Story: Brownstones,
Potato Chips, Black Excellence in 19th Century Brooklyn', *Brownstoner*
magazine, 7 February 2022.

souvenir cardboard boxes: photograph, George S. Bolster Collection.

Thomas Rowlandson's 1811 etching: 'Heres your Potaoes four full Pound for
two pence', from Rowlandson's *Cries of London* series.

A photograph by Eugène Atget: https://bibliotheques-specialisees.paris.fr/
ark:/73873/pf0001827267.

Jean Roubier's photograph: https://bibliotheques-specialisees.paris.fr/
ark:/73873/pf0001809858.

around 10 cents apiece: various sources from Library of Congress
Chronicling America Historic Newspapers.

Thin as tissue paper: Mary Antin, *The Promised Land* (Cambridge, MA:
Riverside Press, 1912).

The word 'snack', hitherto dormant: Oxford English Dictionary.

2. A Twist of Salt

The journey is worth all it costs: Nathan Sheppard, *Saratoga Chips and
Carlsbad Wafers* (New York: Funk & Wagnalls, 1887).

study by Australian scientists: C. M. Smith et al., 'Endogenous Central
Amygdala Mu-Opioid Receptor Signaling Promotes Sodium Appetite in
Mice', *Proceedings of the National Academy of Sciences of the United States
of America*, 113 (2016): 13893–8.

street vendor outside a Paris theatre: James S. Adam, *A Fell Fine Baker: The
Story of United Biscuits* (1974).

unpublished history of Meredith & Drew: H. Marcus Fisk, *Meredith & Drew,
Ltd. Biscuits Manufacturers: A Short History*, circa 1950, courtesy of the
History of Advertising Trust, Norfolk/United Biscuits archive/Pladis.

notes

begin to pick favourites straight off the shelves: various sources, Library of
Congress, Historic American Newspapers

Scott even took a tin of Huntley & Palmers digestives: 'Famous customers',
Huntley & Palmers exhibition, Reading Museum website.

the Pennsylvania Railroad Company issued a booklet: Edwin Adelbert
Rogers (ed.), *Raise Potatoes and Help Win the War* (Philadelphia:
Pennsylvania Department of Agriculture, 1917).

Farmer! Hindenburg calls on you: poster in the Imperial War Museum
collection, Art.IWM PST 7963.

potato mashers: Imperial War Museum weapons and ammunition collection,
MUN 2035.

slicked-back hair and smart suits: 'Smiths Potato Crisps (1929): Another
Record Year Continued Progress and Prosperity Total Distribution of 32½
per cent', *Scotsman*, 18 May 1939, p. 4.

a report in the Middlesex Independent: *County of Middlesex Independent*,
2 November 1935.

Smith's wife Jessie: Dick Weindling and Marianne Colloms, 'Smith's Crisps',
http://kilburnwesthampstead.blogspot.com/2021/08/smiths-crisps.html.

Photographs at Brent Archives: Brent Museum & Archives, object nos 2610, 2611,
2614, https://bma-collections.brent.gov.uk/Details/collectImage/20002550.

first mention of crisps in the Hansard records: Hansard, Tuesday 7 July 1936.

Imperial Crisps Limited: National Archives, Kew.

Prince Harry, enjoys crisps: Prince Harry, *Spare* (London: Bantam Press,
2023), p. 250.

American entrepreneur Laura Scudder: https://laurascudders.com/about-us.

wages had gone up in many heavy industries: Roger Kershaw, 'The Carlisle
Experiment: Limiting Alcohol in Wartime', National Archives blog,
15 January 2015.

Now serving Tayto crisps from behind the bar: as checked by telephone,
6 February 2024.

Inter-war British pubs: Emily Cole, 'The Urban and Suburban Public House
in Inter-War England, 1918–1939', Historic England, 2015.

Children could also be seen waiting: oral history recording undertaken with
John McCarthy as part of the Millennibrum project, Birmingham Archives,
Heritage and Photography Service, MS 2255/2/37.

mostly sold in the hospitality trade until the 1960s: Alan Bevan, 'The UK
Potato Crisp Industry, 1960–72: A Study of New Entry Competition',
Journal of Industrial Economics, 22 (1974): 281–97.

'The Man Who Ate Spain': Cróna Gallagher, 'The Man Who Ate Spain',
Prairie Schooner, 87 (2013): 29–39.

newsreel from 1957: 'Crunch: Northumbria', http://bufvc.ac.uk/
newsonscreen/search/index.php/story/345979.

the symbolic significance of salt: Ernest Jones, 'The Symbolic Significance of
Salt in Folklore and Superstition', in *Essays in Applied Psycho-analysis*, vol.
2 (London: Hogarth Press/Institute of Psycho-analysis, 1921).

Matthew Bailey, professor of renal physiology: interview, 6 March 2023.

Salt was a cooking 'spice' in medieval times: Peter Brears et al., *A Taste of
History: 10,000 Years of Food in Britain* (London: English Heritage in
association with British Museum Press, 1993).

salt-reduction programme conducted by the Chinese government in 2007:
Shuai Shao et al., 'Salt Reduction in China: A State-of-the-Art Review',
Risk Management and Healthcare Policy, 10 (2017): 17–28.

relevant patent statement: https://patents.google.com/patent/
WO2022155477A1/en?q=chromovert&assignee=Secondcell+Bio %2c+Llc.

Stephen Roper: interview, 9 May 2023.

As few as three decades ago, taste buds: Stephen D. Roper, 'Taste Buds as
Peripheral Chemosensory Processors', *Seminars in Cell & Developmental
Biology*, 24 (2013): 71–9.

some of the cell types in the taste buds: A. Taruno et al., 'Taste Transduction
and Channel Synapses in Taste Buds', *Pflügers Archiv* 473 (2021): 3–13.

3. Humble Beginnings

George Duffee: Imperial War Museum, oral history collection, cat. no. 34415.

notes

A US Army Air Force pilot remembered: Robert Honeycutt, https://www.loc. gov/item/afc2001001.20352.

Temporary laws: Ministry of Information trailer, 1945, https://www. britishpathe.com/asset/208243.

1941 annual general meeting: 'Smith's Potato Crisps: Popularity of Product More than Maintained', *Scotsman*, 5 June 1941, p. 2.

When Morgan addressed: 'Smith's Potato Crisps: Incessant Demand. Sir Herbert Morgan's Speech', *Scotsman*, 7 July 1949, p. 3.

Seaman Tom Barker: Imperial War Museum sound collection, cat. no. 21200.

granddaughter, Jennifer Fraser, later recalled a childhood trip: Angie Brown, 'My Grandpa Founded Golden Wonder but I Never Saw Him Eat Crisps', BBC News, 22 October 2022.

gleeful crisp eating: 'Potatoe Chips' by Gladys Carr and Julia Bunora, performed by Slim Gaillard, 1952. Mercury Records.

newsletter, Potato Post: archives accessed in the National Records of Scotland, Edinburgh.

At Smith's AGM in 1950: 'Smith's Potato Crisps: Incessant Demand'.

No, I can't endure them: T. S. Eliot, *The Cocktail Party* (London: Faber & Faber, 1950).

Even as late as 1980: *JS Journal*, March 1980, Sainsbury Archive, https:// www.sainsburyarchive.org.uk.

seasonal delicacy, like oysters: Alfred Woolf, 'Collected, Manufactured and Delivered in 48 Hours', *Commercial Motor*, 3 August 1951, p. 43.

pinpointed by Mr Fisk: Fisk, *Meredith & Drew, Ltd.*

Frito-Lay's annual report proclaimed in 1961: https://archive.org/details/ pepsicofritolayannualreports/fritolay1961.

Frito Co. was started by Charles Elmer Doolin in 1932: *Evening Star*, 23 July 1959.

Lord Dulverton, Imperial's chairman, said in his 1947 AGM review: 'The Imperial Tobacco Co. (of Great Britain and Ireland), Limited: Lord Dulverton's Review', *Scotsman*, 19 March 1947, p. 3.

4. Cheese and Onion

popular Irish actor Paul Mescal discussed his fashion sense: 'Paul Mescal Discusses His Viral Off-Duty Look in Our Latest Episode of Lookbook', *Esquire*/youtube.com, August 2023.

a tiny enterprise brought to life with just £500 by Joseph 'Spud' Murphy: https://taytocrisps.ie/history; Paul Rouse, 'Murphy, Joe', *Dictionary of Irish Biography* (2009).

It was a dump: John Bromley, 'Cloonacool Man Invented Cheese and Onion Crisps', *Sligo Weekender*, 19 August 2021.

Our cheese-and-onion flavour is world famous: 'Tayto Tastes Crisp Success by Post', *Financial Times*, 15 October 1988, p. 5.

Mana . . . had to lay off hundreds of staff, Mònica Bernabé, 'The End of the Afghan Crisp Empire', *Diari Ara*, 30 September 2021.

The dietitian and food technologist: Richard L. M. Synge, 'Nobel Lecture', https://www.nobelprize.org/prizes/chemistry/1952/synge/lecture.

Emma Wood considers all these questions: interviews, 2023.

Ham and cheese and onion Tayto in a Belfast bap: Sophie Gadd and Maurice Fitzmaurice, 'Simply Crispy: World's First Crisp Sandwich Cafe Opens in Belfast', *Irish Mirror Online*, 12 January 2015.

YouGov even put this question to the public: 'What Colour Packs Do You Think the Following Flavours of Crisp SHOULD Be Sold In?', YouGov Survey, fieldwork 24–5 October 2016, https://ygo-assets-websites-editorial-emea.yougov.net/documents/InternalResults_161025_CrispPackagingwithGOR_W.pdf.

warrant a statement on the Walkers website: Brands & flavours FAQ at Walkers.co.uk.

Charles Spence . . . reported: Betina Piqueras-Fiszman and Charles Spence, 'Crossmodal Correspondences in Product Packaging: Assessing Color–Flavor Correspondences for Potato Chips (Crisps), *Appetite*, 57 (2011): 753–7.

Larry Bush, technical manager for Squares at the time, told me: interview, 18 August 2023.

5. Into a Machine

lives on as a fondly remembered ghost in local online message boards: https:// winnershhistoricalsociety.wordpress.com/pictures/vintage.

Una had just mowed her lawn: interview, 7 September 2023.

She ate her first apple on the flight to Heathrow: Una Chandler, *A Long Way from Home* (Kibworth Beauchamp: Matador, 2015).

women born in 1958: B. Roantree and K. Vira, *The Rise and Rise of Women's Employment in the UK* (London: IFS, 2018).

transformative impact on Assam's entire ecosystem: 'PepsiCo India to Establish INR 778 Crore Greenfield Food Plant in Nalbari, Assam', Newsdesk, 6 September 2023.

expanding penetration across the nation: 'PepsiCo and General Mills Expand Footprint in India with New Facilities', *Milling Middle East and Africa*, 8 September 2023.

Delhi High Court decreed: 'Delhi High Court Sets Aside Order Revoking PepsiCo's Potato Patent', *The Hindu*, 11 January 2024.

One man, John Mudd: interview, 27 November 2023.

Walkers wasn't quite a national brand: Glenn, *The Best Job in the World*.

M&S had to apologise in 2023: John Sleigh, 'M and S Making British Potato Crisps Using Non British Tatties', *Scottish Farmer*, 8 August 2023.

Chris Dimelow of PepsiCo's potato and tortilla platform: interview, 30 March 2023.

6. Prawn Cocktail

Delia Smith: Delia Smith, *Complete Cookery Course* (London: Ebury, 1978).

Gerald Kaufman: Hansard, 8 March 1973.

Wing Yip: British Library Oral History collection.

early day motion tabled in Parliament: EDM tabled 30 April 1991.

Dame Jill Knight, in a 1993 Commons debate: Hansard, 23 July 1993.

Boris Johnson: Boris Johnson, 'There Is Only One Way to Get the Change

We Want – Vote to Leave the EU', *Daily Telegraph*, 16 March 2016.

With the rise of incomes: JS *Journal*, February 1964, p. 29, Sainsbury Archive, https://www.sainsburyarchive.org.uk.

Food Safety Act 1990: Food Safety Agency, *The Food Safety Act 1990: A Guide for Businesses* (2009 edition); Food Safety Agency, 'Criteria for the Use of the Terms Fresh, Pure, Natural Etc. in Food Labelling' (revised 2008).

The PepsiCo sale was only possible once the mooted merger: Competition and Markets Authority, 'Anticipated Acquisition by PepsiCo Inc. of Pipers Crisps Limited: Decision on Relevant Merger Situation and Substantial Lessening of Competition', CMA/48/2019.

7. We Lost Things to Gain Things

A hot-oil feed pipe had apparently malfunctioned: '"Devastating" Fire Guts Corby Crisp Factory', BBC Rewind, 2 July 2023.

It has submitted plans to rebuild: https://pa.eastcambs. gov.uk/online-applications/applicationDetails. do?keyVal=QPT9VYGGGHL00&activeTab=summary, East Cambridgeshire District Council, 21/00396/FUM.

The timing was also strategic: Douglas C. McGill, 'Pepsico, to Aid Europe Sales, Buys 2 British Snack Units', *New York Times*, 4 July 1989.

The Leicester factory, Jack said: interview, 22 November 2023.

By 1984, Britons were spending £805 million: P. Clough, 'High Restaurant Prices Blamed for Rise of Snack-Eating Britons', *The Times*, 19 December 1985; D. Fishlock, 'Britons Set to Nibble through a Crisp 1 Billion Pounds a Year', *Financial Times*, 19 February 1985, p. 6.

At the end of the decade: D. Harris, 'British Appetite for Snack Foods Keeps Growing', *The Times*, 3 January 1989.

already received investment to create an automated warehouse: S. Hallahan, 'Robot Go-Slow in the Factory', *The Times*, 25 September 1992.

In 1958, the vast majority of British crisp consumption: Alan Bevan, 'The UK Potato Crisp Industry'.

notes

Golden Wonder saw women as a new customer segment: Golden
Wonder commercial, 1965, https://www.hatads.org.uk/catalogue/
record/94cb11fd-d5a8-4f47-915a-fc6ff12ce4a9.

broadcaster David Frost: *Desert Island Discs*, broadcast 15 April 1963,
https://www.bbc.co.uk/programmes/p009y5gt.

Roy Jenkins: Hansard, 15 April 1969.

Michael Shersby: Hansard, 30 April 1974.

8. Salt and Lineker

The exhibition drew a good crowd: '1980's Crisp Packet Collector
Creating a Media Storm', De La Warr Pavilion blog, https://www.dlwp.
com/1980s-crisp-packet-collector-creating-a-media-storm/.

the Crisp Packet Clutch costs a cool £1,600: price correct as of 20
February 2024, https://www.anyahindmarch.com/products/
crisp-packet-ii-metallic-in-brass-pale-gold.

the best description of Scottish cold: Robert Louis Stevenson, *Kidnapped*
(1886): 'The room was as cold as a well, and the bed, when I had found my
way to it, as damp as a peat-hag.'

as his Irish Times *obituary stated*: 'The King of Irish Crisps Who Realised
His Theme Park Dream against the Odds', *Irish Times*, 18 June 2022.

a fictionalised account of his life: *The Man Inside the Jacket* (Ashbourne:
Tayto, 2009).

Lineker's first piece of work with Walkers: 'Welcome Home', 1994–5,
https://www.hatads.org.uk/catalogue/record/a82fb0d2-051b-4988
-8480-c95eca30b3e0.

Consensus Action on Salt and Health complained: Alexi Mostrous, 'Walkers
Crisps Salt Claim Criticised by Watchdog', *Guardian*, 16 August 2006.

relaxation scheduled nationwide at 5 p.m. on Fridays: Maddy Savage,
'Fredagsmys: The Unlikely Symbol of Sweden's "Cosy Friday"', BBC
Worklife, 28 May 2021.

Spending on junk food advertising: A. O'Dowd, 'Spending on Junk Food Advertising Is Nearly 30 Times What Government Spends on Promoting Healthy Eating', *British Medical Journal*, 11 October 2017.

devil's buttermilk: Lower Bann Voices oral history interview with Nigel Flynn, March 2022, Northern Ireland Community Archive.

'Shopping Generation' survey: Ed Mayo, 'Shopping Generation', *Young Consumers*, 6 (2005): 43–9.

new food-based standards: Education (Nutritional Standards for School Lunches) (England) Regulations 2006.

phased out the presence of branded crisps: 'Hospital Vending Machines: Helping People Make Healthier Choices', Public Health England, 2018.

recent Government Office for Science review: 'Tackling Obesities: Future Choices – Obesogenic Environments – Evidence Review', Government Office for Science, 2007.

Atul owns a Londis grocery store in Harefield: interview, 14 July 2023.

In his memoir: Joe Coulombe and Patty Civalleri, *Becoming Trader Joe: How I Did Business My Way and Still Beat the Big Guys* (New York: HarperCollins, 2021).

Wallace Waite used to ask his family: Judy Faraday, 'Mr Waite's Style of Marketing', Waitrose & Partners Memory Store, 2018.

9. Pickled Fish

Clare Scott Dryden: interview, 4 December 2023.

according to his obituary: 'Fallece César Bonilla, capitán de unas patatas de Óscar', *La Voz de Galicia*, 16 February 2024.

delicious Mexican crispie: *Brownsville Herald*, 23 July 1934.

Mikesell purchased some potato-chip equipment: *Dayton Union News*, 27 May 1942.

Laura Bounds is the sole director of Kent Crisps: interview, 30 August 2023.

10. Fieldwork

Tim Rooke is a man who has spent a lifetime: interviews, June 2023.

The trends up to 2020 showed a very slight incline: 'GB Planted Area by Sector', AHDB Horticulture and Potatoes website.

inadequacy of life on Earth: Cadbury's Smash Commercial, 1973, https://www.hatads.org.uk/catalogue/record/f1e6fe4b-ba95-4ca9 -b711-f75eed5d22be.

David Foster Wallace once said of the lobster: in 'Consider the Lobster' (2004), reprinted in *Consider the Lobster and Other Essays* (New York: Little, Brown, 2005).

Chris Dimelow . . . told me: interview, op. cit.

acrylamide in starchy foods was discovered: Hans Lingnert et al., 'Acrylamide in Food: Mechanisms of Formation and Influencing Factors during Heating of Foods', *Scandinavian Journal of Nutrition*, 46 (2002): 159–72.

paper published in the Journal of Experimental Botany: Nigel G. Halford et al., 'The Acrylamide Problem', *Journal of Experimental Botany*, 63 (2012): 2841–51.

Epilogue

'*Ode to French Fries*': Pablo Neruda, *Odas elementales*.

image credits

Page One

A 1930s advertising booklet for Smith's Crisps. The increasing popularity of picnics worked in crisps' favour. *Amoret Tanner / Alamy Stock Photo*

A typical 1940s crisp packet in waxy paper. Early crisps contained no additives – only oil and salt. *Simon Robinson / Easy On The Eye / Alamy Stock Photo*

Page Two

Marilyn Monroe and Tom Ewell with a cameo from a bag of Bell's Potato Chips in *The Seven Year Itch* (1955). *Photo 12 / Alamy Stock Photo*

Page Three

A family picnic in New England, 1958, with a bag of State Line Potato Chips. The brand's Connecticut birthplace, Enfield, neighboured Massachusetts. *Kirn Vintage Stock / Alamy Stock Photo*

Page Four

A 1950s advert for Seabrook Crisps, based in Bradford. Different areas of the UK have flavour preferences. Salt and vinegar, for example, is hugely popular in Scotland. *Simon Robinson / Alamy Stock Photo*

Page Five

A worker at the Golden Wonder warehouse in Bothwell, 1970. The boxes promise a special offer of 'free tights'; it was then common among crisp brands to flaunt gifts and toys that could be exchanged for packet coupons. *Trinity Mirror / Mirrorpix / Alamy Stock Photo*

A 1970s English pub session. Public houses were once crisps' biggest marketplace. *Allan Cash Picture Library / Alamy Stock Photo*

Page Six

A delivery of Ready Salted crisps to the village shop in St Just, Cornwall, 1970. Delivery drivers often doubled up as salesmen. *Homer Sykes / Alamy Stock Photo*

Mary Berry on a panel judging specimens of crisp, 1977. *Trinity Mirror / Mirrorpix / Alamy Stock Photo*

Page Seven

A 1969 advert for Golden Wonder, which started as a sideline to an Edinburgh bakery in 1947. *Neil Baylis / Alamy Stock Photo*

Page Eight

A persuasive beer mat. Advertising became the toughest battleground of the so-called 'crisp wars'. *Tegestology / Alamy Stock Photo*

Former England footballer Gary Lineker in a promotion for Walkers Crisps in 1994. *PA Images / Alamy Stock Photo*

postscript

Tempting as it was to become a crisp influencer, no free crisps were consumed or solicited in the writing of this book.